IRRESISTIBLE BLURBS

IRRESISTIBLE BLURBS

HOW TO WRITE
A BOOK DESCRIPTION
ROMANCE READERS
WILL LOVE

SIRI CALDWELL

Brussels Sprout Press

Irresistible Blurbs:
How to Write a Book Description
Romance Readers Will Love

Cover design by EVING, Eva Veber s. p.

ISBN: 978-0-9974023-5-3 (paperback)
ISBN: 978-0-9974023-4-6 (ebook)

Brussels Sprout Press
P.O. Box 42133
Arlington, VA 22204
United States of America

First edition, revised December 2024
First published May 2020

CONTENTS

PART I

GETTING FOCUSED

Subgenres

Tropes

Keywords

Details

1

INTRODUCTION

This book is geared to indie authors who write their own book description or sales copy—what we referred to back in the pre-ebook days as the back cover copy or dust jacket copy and now fondly nickname the blurb.

If you have a traditional publisher, someone on your editorial team will write this for you and most likely will not appreciate your input. It's possible this person might steal a few lines from your synopsis to slap on the back cover, but this book is not about how to craft paragraphs your editor will be tempted to call her own. It's about writing great descriptions that sell books to *readers*, not to acquiring editors.

Most of the advice you'll read here can be applied to any type of fiction, but my focus is romance novels. I write romance, I love romance, and I believe romance sales copy deserves to be treated as a topic all its own, not brushed off as "Do what you'd do for a thriller, but with two protagonists." The romance genre is not an afterthought—not here. All the examples and all the details in this book are romance-specific.

You'll learn how to target your audience with genre-specific cues, how to maximize your description's impact by choosing the right details, and how to structure the whole thing in a number of traditional and not-so-traditional ways.

No matter how wonderful your book is, no one will take the chance to find out if you scare them off with a boring, blah, or confusing description.

So let's fix that and get your book into readers'—buyers'—hands!

A BLURB IS NOT A SYNOPSIS

If you're coming to indie publishing from traditional publishing, you've queried agents or editors, which involves sending them a synopsis.

A synopsis can be one to ten pages or more. It explains the plot in detail and must reveal how the story ends. Basically, the synopsis saves your acquiring editor or agent the effort of having to read your book. This is her job, and she has 47 other submissions to read by next Thursday, and she has a headache just thinking about it. If you can't prove to her in three pages that you're capable of writing a plot that makes sense, she will delete your manuscript with a clear conscience and move on.

Readers are different. For them, reading your book is not a job they have to slog through under deadline. Readers don't want you to spoil what happens. They don't want to know the ending before they've read the beginning.

What *do* they want? They want to get excited about your story's potential. They want to be intrigued.

So, how do you intrigue them? By *not* telling them everything. By hinting, and raising compelling questions, and then shutting up. Usually, by explaining the setup—

the beginning of the book—and nothing more.

If they want to know what happens next, they'll have to buy the book.

That's how it works.

Readers definitely won't stick around for a three-page summary to decide whether they'll like your book. You'll be lucky if they have the patience to read three paragraphs. Even three sentences. If you don't catch their interest immediately, they'll bail.

You need to make them care enough about your story to read past the first sentence. You do that by making them feel. Curiosity...concern...amusement...anything. People read fiction, especially romance, because they want an emotional experience.

A list of plot points does not create an emotional experience. A just-the-facts-ma'am book report does not create a mood. (Not unless you count boredom.)

So don't think of your blurb as a summary of the plot. You don't need to explain who all the characters are. You don't need to explain all the subplots. Or even much of the main plot. That's hopeless.

Instead, think of your book description as an advertisement.

Because it is.

And what's the first thing you need to do when you write an ad? You need to know what it is you're selling, and know who you're selling it to. What that translates to for novels is what I'm going to talk about next: knowing your subgenre.

2

KNOW YOUR SUBGENRE

Hang out with romance authors and you'll quickly learn all about romance subgenres.

Honestly, I used to have no idea. As a reader, I read the authors I liked and didn't think much about what category those books fell into. With some exceptions (African American romances shelved with African American literature instead of in the romance section; LGBTQ romances unavailable outside of gay bookstores), shops sold it all under the banner of romance, separating out only the oversized hardbacks and trade paperbacks and undersized Harlequins, which were displayed in their own spinner racks. My local library didn't even have a romance section (and still doesn't); it was all shelved alphabetically by author under "fiction".

Then I finished writing my first book and joined my local chapter of Romance Writers of America, and the first thing everyone asked me was, "What do you write?"

"Um," I said. "Romance?"

Was this a trick question?

No. It was not a trick question. These ladies were dead serious.

And you should be, too.

Because from a marketing standpoint, there is a world of difference between a sweet Christian inspirational romance and a post-apocalyptic romantic suspense. In this online age, hardcore romance readers are usually well aware of what, for example, the term *contemporary romance* means, and it's easy for them to browse by category, either by using keywords or by taking advantage of the way online booksellers "shelve" books by subgenre.

I could now go on and on explaining the differences that define these subgenres, but I won't waste your time, since I'm sure you already know which subgenre your book fits into.

But if you don't, and you're not sure what the options are, go to the Book Industry Study Group website (bisg.org) and click on their "Complete BISAC Subject Headings List". (BISAC stands for Book Industry Standards and Communications, an industry standard for bookstore shelving and database searching.)

Or go to your favorite online bookseller's website, which may provide a menu of romance categories including contemporary romance, erotic romance, fantasy romance (romantasy), historical romance, inspirational romance, romantic mystery, paranormal romance, romantic comedy, romantic suspense, science fiction romance, and more.

Most of these can have subcategories. Historical romance, for example, can be broken down by time period and geography. Paranormal romance can be subdivided by supernatural element.

Many subcategories of course overlap, especially when it comes to go-anywhere niches like holiday romance, medical romance, military romance, and sports romance, or identities like young adult.

Amazon, BISAC, the Library of Congress, WorldCat,

and their ilk are certainly not the final word on which romance subgenres deserve their own label or how they should be defined, but their categories are useful to keep in mind.

Why bother with this exercise?

The one-word answer? Marketing.

Know *what* you're selling so you know *how* to sell it.

You'll have to do this in any case, because assigning a standard BISAC-based category or two is part of the process when you put your book up for sale on any bookseller's website.

But just as importantly, you'll want to keep your subgenre in mind when you're writing your description so you can include genre-specific cues which help readers identify whether your book is *their* kind of book.

TROPES

Readers like their genres. They like their subgenres. They like their tropes.

What's a trope? It's like a sub-subgenre. (The line is blurry.)

(Some authors argue about terminology, but for marketing purposes, those arguments are irrelevant. Is hockey romance a subgenre? A hook? A trope? Who cares?)

A trope is a familiar type of story or specific story element that has built-in reader expectations. Tropes provide an immediately identifiable anchor in a sea of choices, and they play a huge role in the romance genre.

Sometimes a trope is defined by the character's job,

role, or identity:

>best man
>duke
>firefighter
>girl next door
>ice queen
>mail-order bride
>millionaire
>rancher
>rock star
>succubus
>surgeon
>telepath
>wedding planner

Or a pair of characters:

>business rivals
>cat and mouse (law enforcement officer/lawbreaker)
>fated mates
>governess/widower
>grumpy/sunshine
>housemates
>jock/nerd
>May/December
>virgin/rake

Other times a trope is defined by the conflict:

>alien abduction
>enemies to lovers
>fake fiancé(e)
>friends to lovers

instant family
interplanetary political intrigue
marooned together
mistaken identity
second chance at love
time travel
unexpected pregnancy

Or even a setting:

small town
workplace

Not every novel is structured around a trope—nor should it be—so don't worry if you can't identify one for your book. But if you *can*, you'll want to make it clear what the main trope is. If a reader is, for example, a marriage-of-convenience junky, you won't have to work too hard to pique his interest in your marriage-of-convenience plot, so take advantage of that.

While you're at it, the book description is not the only place where you should indicate your trope and/or subgenre. The book description, the title, the cover design, the keywords, and the categories all work together to convey what your book is about and give your readers familiar signposts they recognize—signposts that say:

You know me.

You like me.

You want me.

START WITH THE RIGHT FOUNDATION

It may seem as though knowing your genre/sub-genre/sub-subgenre/trope/category would be intuitive and obvious and hardly worth mentioning. Yet this is where I went wrong with one of my novels, and it's what prompted me to do the research that ultimately led me to write this how-to book.

It's why I can tell you from personal experience that it all starts here. Get the subgenre wrong, get the tone wrong, and the whole blurb is doomed.

With *Mistletoe Mishap*, I'd written a blurb I loved, and I'd gotten good feedback on it from writer friends.

Then the reviews came in.

Readers said they were surprised they enjoyed the book, considering the off-putting summary. That the story wasn't what they expected. That the blurb made the book sound trashy, when it was so much more.

Which was shocking.

Shockingly helpful, actually.

My problem was that I thought I'd written an erotic romance. From my point of view, the plot centered on a sexual competition, and that seemed to me to fit the academic or literary definition of this subgenre, which is that the relationship evolves as the result of a series of sexual encounters. In a "regular" romance, by contrast, the relationship develops as the result of other things. Sex may occur, but it doesn't drive the story.

The thing is, readers have their own definition, and it's basically this: erotic romance is the same thing as erotica, and erotica means lots and lots of sex, in lots and lots of graphic detail.

I knew my book didn't have much graphic content. I *knew* it didn't. But I ignored that voice in my head because I wanted to go with *my* definition, not theirs. I liked my definition better! I was right and they were wrong!

And you know what? You know how they say the customer is always right? Yup, the reader is always right.

I'd written a description that fit the genre I believed my book belonged in. The readers disagreed. The book did not sell well.

Readers wrote in their reviews that my book was about a caring, long-term relationship. They wrote that the sex was tame. They wrote that it was *not* erotica.

I grumbled to myself that they didn't understand. I griped that the plot was the plot and there *was* no other way to describe it. I spent weeks in denial before I could say, *Okay, fine.*

Then I rewrote the description.

Out went the unbuttoning of her blouse; in went a shared coffee.

Not because I was pandering to my readers or selling out, but because they were right. My book *was* about those other things. About how relationships change over time, and how differences don't have to drive people apart, and how people reveal certain things about themselves in some contexts while hiding them in others. Those themes were so glaringly obvious to me that I'd ignored them in favor of the technicalities of the plot's structure—and couldn't see where I'd gone wrong until I'd taken a step back.

As a result, I learned three things:

Take-home message number one: Trust that readers know what they want. Disagree with them at your peril.

Take-home message number two: When you're too

close to the book (or its blurb), you may not be the best judge of how it will be perceived.

Take-home message number three: If your book isn't selling, or you're getting reviews that say the book was not what the reader expected, you need to change the description.

About that third point: I ended up changing my description for that book four times. Yeah, sure, the old blurbs still lurk on the internet on sites that picked up whichever version I was publicizing at the time, but so what? No one's going to notice. And if they do happen to notice? Is that not-very-interesting discrepancy going to affect whether they buy my book? No.

And yes, the paperback kept the original back cover copy for a long time because it didn't seem worth it to pay my cover designer to change it until I was sure I'd hit on the version I was going to stick with, but so what? Yes, I regret that my not-so-perfect first attempt shipped to readers' homes, but as an indie author, print copies of my book do not sit on physical shelves in bricks-and-mortar bookstores, so the back cover copy on my paperback plays no role in selling the book. A reader will only see the cover copy *after* they've bought the book, and by that point it doesn't matter anymore.

Unless they see it and are so repelled that they return the book for a refund? Ugh, let's pretend that doesn't happen. Really, it doesn't.

I'll go out on a limb and say if you're in this situation and the only place your books are for sale is online, your back cover could be blank. It's nice to have the description there because it looks professional and it provides information, but let's be real: it's no longer a sales tool.

3

CROSSING GENRES

When your plot straddles multiple genres or subgenres, you have a crucial decision to make: which facet to focus on in your description. The answer will guide you in selecting which details to include.

(And not just for the blurb! This applies to the cover, too. They both work together.)

If you've written a story about Amish sweethearts who chase down a kidnapper, who is your target audience? Inspirational romance readers or suspense readers?

Is your brutally handsome Viking werewolf going to appeal more to fans of paranormal romance or historical romance?

I know you want to say both.

But it's better to choose. Yes, mention the werewolves *and* the Vikings *and* the romance, but choose. Otherwise you'll get reviews that complain there's too much stupid kissing. Or too much unnecessary violence. Or not enough historical detail—and what was the point of all that biting?

Choosing allows you to manage reader expectations by emphasizing one aspect of the plot and appealing first and foremost to your primary readership.

You already know how to do this!

Imagine you run into a friend and she asks what's going on in your life. If this happens at a dinner party, you might bring up a frustrating interaction at work. At the playground, you'll talk about your kids. At your college reunion, you might mention a run-in with a former classmate. There are hundreds of things you could potentially say about your life, but you don't mention them all. You tell one or two anecdotes you think your friend will be interested in.

Tailoring your book description to your audience works the same way. The plot (just like your life) provides many building blocks, and you cannot use them all. Choose the best ones for the situation.

Consider this holiday/young adult/paranormal/romantic suspense:

> It could have been worse. That spell could have turned him into a helpless toad. Yes, he ended up with a weirdly square face, but he still has his powerful sword arm and his regal self-confidence, and it hasn't been a bad life…until now. A battle is raging, the Mouse King is winning, and the Nutcracker Prince may not live to see dawn…or to protect the girl of his dreams from becoming the Mouse King's next victim.

Here I decided to appeal primarily to thriller readers rather than romance readers. That's why the romance plot gets less than a sentence (*to protect the girl of his dreams*), while most of the blurb describes the danger the characters are in, with a little bit of the paranormal aspect thrown in at the beginning.

If I decided instead to target the romance audience, I'd spend more time on the romantic relationship and less time on the fighting-for-their-lives danger. Like this:

Her parents' annual Christmas Eve party is a time to be polite and well-behaved...not for Clara to swoon over a boy her parents wouldn't approve of. They want her to marry one of their friends' sons, not a silent, wooden-faced soldier...even one who moves with the courtly grace and royal bearing of a prince. But when magic sweeps through her home at the stroke of midnight and giant homicidal mice attack, Clara is faced with a life-changing choice: run, or join forces with the mysterious soldier to stop the Mouse King.

Or what about the YA aspect? I could focus on that instead, like this:

Glamorous parties, fabulous dresses, expensive gifts...I should be happy. I just wish my parents would treat me like an adult instead of a cute accessory. They'll never approve of me running off with the soldier I met on Christmas Eve, but I'm doing it. Because I love him. He says the battlefield is no place for a girl like me, but I'm going to prove him wrong. I'm going to protect him, and he's going to protect me, and I won't be scared, because when I'm with him, life is sugar-plum sweet.

Same plot. Three different approaches. Know your audience and write for *them*.

4

INCORPORATE KEYWORDS

When customers search online for their favorite subgenre or trope, they type in keywords such as *space opera romance*, and the search engine does its thing and spits out suggestions.

How do you get your book to show up in those results?

In terms of landing search hits, the power position is the title. Too many online booksellers don't offer keyword searching at all, so on those sites the title has even more weight. That's why you'll see titles like these:

Falling for Her Brother's Best Friend
The Highlander's Wicked Wager
Love in a Small Town
The Royal Bodyguard's Secret Baby
A SEAL for Christmas
Snowbound with the Cowboy
Winning the Billionaire's Heart

Overdo this, and certain people will have snarky, mean things to say about your title, but in a world where search engines rule, it's a technique to consider.

A less clunky approach is to embed keywords that actual humans, rather than computers, will understand.

Consider these examples:

Optimized for computers: *The Bodyguard*
Obvious to humans: *Guarding Anya*
Obvious to humans: *His to Protect*

Optimized for computers: *Werewolves Only*
Obvious to humans: *Howling at the Moon*
Obvious to humans: *Alpha's Mate*

Optimized for computers: *The Reunion*
Obvious to humans: *Not Quite Over You*
Obvious to humans: *Back in Her Arms*

You might find that approach—being trope-y but not *too* trope-y—to be an appealing compromise.

But you don't have to do that, either. There's nothing wrong with giving your book an artistic, more sophisticated title. Beautiful titles make the world a better place.

No matter what, though, do make it easy for potential buyers to quickly identify what type of story it is—if not from the title, then from the cover design and the description—and lead them to your book by using good keywords in the keyword field, if there is one.

When you provide keywords in the keyword field to an online retailer, customers don't see those keywords; they benefit only indirectly when they type one of your terms into the search bar and are shown your book. That means the only way for them to know your book is about, say, lifeguards, is for you to communicate that in the parts they do see—your book description, title, or cover—where this information works in the search engine that is the reader's brain. As she reads your description and comes across these cues, they help her decide whether your book is the kind of book she'll like.

Your heroine is a lifeguard? If lifeguards are an auto-buy, or an auto-no-thanks-I-hate-reading-about-people-in-bikinis, or even just a hmm-that-could-be-interesting, readers want to know. That holds true not only for obvious keywords like the heroine's job, but for less obvious keywords as well, such as *slow burn*—a popular search term which provides important information but is unlikely to be clear from a description of the plot.

In scientific journals, authors are instructed to list relevant keywords at the end of their paper's abstract (equivalent to our blurb)—or an editor or algorithm does it for them—and the way they do it is blunt. It looks like this:

Keywords: Pennsylvania, United States, ground-water, nitrates, phosphates, nutrients, fertilizers, atrazine, herbicides, agriculture, pollution

Sadly, the world of fiction does not value this straightforward approach. Instead, we novelists are expected to be coy. We can't come right out and say:

Keywords: lifeguard, lifesaver, rescuer, beach, seaside, seashore, workplace romance, coworkers, colleagues, hot, steamy, summer fling

(Well, I shouldn't say *can't*. You can do whatever the retailers let you get away with. And by the way, it's a violation of Amazon's terms of service.)

Fiction is all about casting a spell and setting a mood

and drawing readers in. Suddenly encountering undis-guised metadata is likely to break the spell and possibly even confuse people. Better to be subtle and sneak it in.

Brainstorm a list of keywords, both the obvious computer-oriented ones and the more subtle human-oriented ones, and see if you can include some of them in your description without sounding awkward.

Will this improve discoverability?

Possibly.

When keywords in the book description match or complement keywords in the keyword field, this reinforces what the book is about and may boost the book's ranking on Amazon for that keyword.

It may also play a role in how Amazon assigns your book to additional categories you did not select—a process which can either be wonderful or go very, very wrong.

The issue is that these keyword-seeking systems do not understand words in context. They single-mindedly identify certain individual words and phrases that they deem important, then use them to jump to their own conclusions.

Consider this example:

> His mistakes haunt him. He doesn't have a ghost of a chance of winning her back, but the specter of living without her is unbearable.

Haunt, ghost, specter... Take those words out of context, and at this rate, your second-chance romance is going to sound like a ghost story and be offered to the wrong readers.

Don't give the bots the opportunity to misinterpret

your book. Beat them at their own game.

(For examples of appropriately chosen novel-specific words, see Chapter 5: *Be Specific*.)

In addition to guiding automated systems to correctly categorize your book, there are other reasons to deliberately work keywords into your description.

As I already mentioned, they provide important cues to the potential buyer as he reads the description.

Camouflaged keywords may also help readers find your book outside of AmazonLand. For example, Google.

Also book review sites, which usually allow full-text searching. That means there's a search bar which can be used to locate any word used anywhere on the site, so if your blurb appears on the site (either because you provided the description to the reviewer or they copied it from elsewhere), every word you put in your description can be landed on.

Even book review sites that don't offer full-text searching benefit from keyword-oriented word choice if they organize their reviews by category, as it's likely the reviewer (not you) will be choosing the category and keywords with which to tag your book. People are susceptible to suggestion. As long as you're not too far out of step with the reviewer's own perceptions, they'll see your words right in front of them and think, *Oh, the author calls this a hidden identity plot. It was, wasn't it? Perhaps I should tag this book as* hidden identity *rather than* secrets & lies *and* masquerade. When that happens, it means incorporating the subgenre, tropes, and keywords into the description helps get your book in front of the right readers—by nudging the reviewer toward your preferred tags.

Reader communities such as Goodreads work the same way. Readers tag the books they're interested in with phrases that function as keywords or categories and help other people discover your book. If you want to be found under a more discoverable keyphrase than *all the feels*, *super cute*, or *favorite couples*, the words you choose to use in your description can steer readers toward something more helpful (albeit less adorably flattering).

5

BE SPECIFIC

Have you ever received a (presumably) targeted ad for a book where you thought, *Wow. Why do they think I'd want to read that*?

Perhaps it was a romance between two doctors who work side by side at the hospital late into the night, and you've never bought a medical romance in your life. (Except for that one you once picked up at a used book sale back in 1995 and are still miffed that you spent 50 cents on.)

Is it *possible* you might branch out and try something new? Of course.

Is it *likely*? Not really.

My goal is not to reach a million readers. My goal is to reach readers who will love my books. There will never be a book that everyone in the world will like. There is no romance novel that all romance readers will like. Even mega-bestsellers are hated by significant swaths of the reading population. So aside from the fact that it's easy to claim I don't want something that'll never happen anyway, I would very much rather not reach readers who will hate my books and give me bad reviews. When readers find what they're looking for, everyone's happy.

Booksellers are matchmakers, and the blurb is a book's dating profile. Being vague in an attempt to reach a broad audience helps no one. (True for both books and singles searching for love.)

Consider this dating profile:

> I enjoy travel, going out with friends, and relaxing at home with takeout pizza.

Are you intrigued?

I'm not.

This description tells me nothing about the person. (If I'm being generous I'll admit it tells me they're not a recluse and they're not gluten intolerant. Which only interests me if I'm on the rebound from my ex who hated traveling and made rude comments about how I loved to bake my own challah, and now I'm specifically trying to avoid such people.)

This trying-to-appeal-to-everyone behavior shows up in book descriptions like this one:

> Martin is a successful attorney, but he's always yearned for more.

Oh, Martin. Such a cliché.

I want to know something unique about this guy. (Actually, I don't, because I'm bored already. And I kind of have no sympathy for him. But let's pretend I do.)

How about this:

> Martin Jones, Esquire, never has time for anything but his current caseload. He certainly doesn't have time to detour from his commute every evening to drop off a single shirt at the dry cleaner's.

Now Martin's become a bit of a weirdo. And now I might want to know more.

Or I might decide this book is not for me.

Which is good news! You want to scare away potential buyers who won't like your writing. If they don't buy your book, they won't give you one-star reviews. (Or maybe they will anyway. Some people suck.)

If you clearly understand what subgenre and/or trope your book falls into, and clearly communicate that to your audience, and don't try to sell your book to everyone in the world with vague generalities you hope will appeal to everyone, your book will sound interesting because it will be unique. It will be a love story between a germophobic patent attorney and the clerk at the dry cleaner's who invents cleaning gadgets, rather than a romance between two friendly people who enjoy sharing meals and end up falling in love.

The thing is, vague is boring.

Details are interesting.

But save your details for things that matter. Make them count.

Knowing the heroine sports an elaborate dinosaur tattoo etched across the delicate slope of her kissable neck and the sharp angle of her bared shoulder blade? A tattoo designed by a renowned artist trained on the alien planet Triceratopia? These details might catch the reader's attention with their foreignness, but a character's *looks* do not tell us anything about *who she is*.

Really, how many times do we have to read that the hero encountered a beautiful flame-haired lass? Her beauty and her hair color are the most interesting things you could come up with to say about your heroine?

Please.

Feel free to describe your characters' hotness at length in the novel itself, but in the book description, you don't have a lot of words to make a strong impression. Save them for something more important.

Like what?

Anything that makes your characters come alive or heightens the conflict is in the running.

Specifics that showcase your subgenre are also important. Is your book a romantic comedy? Make the reader laugh. A dreamy historical romance? Make her swoon. A romantic thriller? Amp up the suspense.

And always remember the book description is your potential reader's first—and perhaps only—introduction to your writing voice. So show it off! Be your best self, but be yourself. Don't write a blurb that sounds like another book's blurb you happen to like. Give it your own style. If you're having trouble with this, you might be jealous of traditionally published authors who have a professional editor to do it for them, but don't be. You have an advantage over them: Your blurb will sound like *you*. If you let it.

Character. Conflict. Subgenre. Voice.

These are the elements I'll come back to again and again.

Plot is not.

And yet most book descriptions may look, on the surface, as if they're explaining the plot.

They're not. (Well, some are.)

You can't just outline a sequence of events and hope they sound interesting because of course they're interesting and that's what happens in the book and the book is great.

Outlines are boring.

No one wants you to explain what happens. They want you to make them laugh, or interest them in the characters, or make them wonder how an untenable situation will be resolved.

And details are key to accomplishing this.

Our attorney with the dry cleaning problem is an example of detail illuminating character.

How does detail increase conflict? As an example, here's something I rewrote for the worse:

> In 1944, Dorothy Fairfax works for Britain's Women's Royal Naval Service piecing together photographs to create maps of Normandy. She collaborates closely with Lt. Wyatt Paxton, an American naval officer, who will base the Allies' bombardment plans on her work.

It's so much stronger like this:

> In 1944, American naval officer Lt. Wyatt Paxton arrives in London to prepare for the Allied invasion of France. He works closely with Dorothy Fairfax, a "Wren" in the Women's Royal Naval Service. Dorothy pieces together reconnaissance photographs with thousands of holiday snapshots of France—including those of her own family's summer home—in order to create accurate maps of Normandy. Maps that Wyatt will turn into naval bombardment plans.

> (*The Sea Before Us* by Sarah Sundin)

Why is this longer, more detailed approach better? Because, although war is of course conflict, it's so big and overwhelming that it's paradoxically less interesting than a single human being's problems. The mention that Dorothy's family owns a summer home in Normandy makes the larger threat personal. Her private photos—from a happier past—are being weaponized. Her home is in the hands of the enemy, and she's helping to bomb it. Without this detail, there's much less impact—even though the larger conflict (the war) remains.

Another way to think about how much detail to include is to frame it as a question of showing versus telling—typically referred to as "show, don't tell"—something every writer has lots of practice with.

By necessity, your description will involve a lot of telling—after all, you don't have much space—but that doesn't mean you don't have a little room to show.

Here I go again with a bad rewrite:

> James "Iceman" Bracelyn has a stressful life. In addition to being CEO of Ponderosa Resort, he's also guardian of the family's biggest secrets.

That's informative but blah. Instead we have this:

> James "Iceman" Bracelyn is wound tighter than a vintage Rolex. Besides his CEO role at Ponderosa Resort, he's guardian of the family's biggest secrets, including a doozy that keeps him up at night. Alone. In that big bed he'd rather not share, thank you very much.
>
> (*Stiff Suit* by Tawna Fenske)

Telling: *James has a stressful life.*

Showing: *[His stressful life] keeps him up at night.*

The size of his bed? That's completely nonessential to understanding the plot, but it gives James some personality and provides an opportunity to showcase the writer's voice.

And what about that Rolex? Sure, it's a vivid way to say he's tense—so, *so* much better than "James is tense" or "James can't relax"—but doesn't it contradict my rant about describing characters' physical appearance? No, because the Rolex is not just about what he wears, it's about his social status, which highlights the trope (wealthy, powerful businessman), which is one of the prime goals of the blurb.

To be fair, that Triceratopia tattoo does signal subgenre (extraterrestrial science fiction or fantasy) and can be considered world-building, but it uses way too many words to do so. The wristwatch is more powerful because it does double duty, evoking the trope while describing the protagonist's emotional state in a minimal number of words.

Here's another example of how adding a single key detail can make a dramatic difference:

> Putting down roots in this town again is not Kyle's plan. As soon as he can, he's taking his daughter and her princess costumes and moving on.
>
> (*The Pick Up* by Allison Temple)

Those princess costumes tell us so much, not only about Kyle's daughter, but also about him.

STRONG WRITING AND WORD CHOICE

Being specific is about more than which details you choose to include; it's also about wording. Choosing strong nouns and verbs, using active (not passive) voice, and selecting words that resonate with your unique plot will strengthen your writing and give your words greater impact.

Strong nouns and verbs

> **Weak:** Her dog
> **Strong:** Her Chihuahua

> **Weak:** jumps up from a nap, barking wildly,
> **Strong:** erupts in a frenzy of barking

> **Weak:** and runs after
> **Strong:** and chases

> **Weak:** the man who's breaking into her house.
> **Strong:** the intruder.

Weak words paint a generic picture and require you to use more words than necessary as you pile on details to explain what you mean.

Strong words communicate more with less, allowing you to get your message across clearly and quickly in a limited amount of space.

Active versus passive voice

> Passive voice: The contract has not yet been signed.

> Active voice: My director has not yet signed the contract.

What's the difference? In passive voice, things just...happen. *Why* they happen is glossed over. In active voice, someone or something is identified as the responsible party.

In this example, our administrative assistant doesn't want to look like she's accusing her boss of being inefficient (never mind admitting he hasn't set foot in the office all week because it's been beautiful golfing weather), so she avoids any mention of *who* was supposed to sign. The signature is missing, but it's not anyone's fault.

This may be a useful skill in a drama-filled office, but in writing book descriptions, tact is not rewarded. You want to draw attention to your characters' behavior, not hide it behind a veneer of politeness.

Unless, of course, you are withholding information on purpose.

If you're intentionally helping your villain slither away unseen, then by all means, use passive voice:

> Shots were fired.

Novel-specific word choice

Your novel is unique. Your characters have specific jobs, the story explores particular themes, and your tone sets a certain mood. Your description can evoke all these particulars when you choose novel-specific words and appropriate metaphors.

In the following example, the novel is about a former soldier, so the description uses militaristic words (*breaks, armor, task, defending, winning*).

> Once she breaks through his armor, traversing the wilds of the Amazon will prove an easier task than defending himself against her winning charms…
>
> (*Courageous* by Diana Palmer)

In this next one, in keeping with a knitting theme, the character's resolve doesn't *weaken*, it *unravels*.

> The more time he spends with Jenna, the more his resolve begins to unravel…
>
> (*Loves Me, Loves Me Knot* by Heidi Betts)

Dogs? Here, a leash is used as a metaphor, and the word *instincts* is appropriately animalistic.

> When it comes to training K-9 patrol dogs, Yardley Summers always trusts her instincts. But when it comes to dating men, she keeps her heart on a very short leash.
>
> (*Rival Forces* by D. D. Ayres)

A snowboarder and a skier: *steeper, collide, breakneck speed*.

> The stakes become steeper than any mountain either of them will ever face when legacies and hearts collide at breakneck speed.
>
> (*Edge of Glory* by Rachel Spangler)

A dancer: *spinning*.

> The truth sends her spinning straight into the arms of the man she never knew she'd always wanted.
>
> (*With a Twist* by Staci Hart)

Here, an athlete's attraction is likened to his need for calories—not merely *the lunch buffet*, but *the lunch buffet after practice*.

> Jason wants me, but he won't admit it. That man looks at me the way a hockey player eyes the lunch buffet after practice—and I love it.
>
> (*Overnight Sensation* by Sarina Bowen)

In this final example, the description could have ended with a generic line: *Will Tara get married?* Instead, it's phrased in a way that's specific to the character, who is an investigator for the Internal Revenue Service.

> When Tara snatches the bridal bouquet and her boyfriend Nick catches the satin garter, could Tara's days of filing single tax returns be over?
>
> (*Death, Taxes, and a Satin Garter* by Diane Kelly)

I'll talk about novel-specific word choice again in Chapter 8: *Supercharge the Ending,* with examples of the important role it can play in the very last line.

PART II

GETTING IT DONE

Tagline

Opening

Ending

Structure

Extras

6

TANTALIZE WITH A TAGLINE

There are three places in the book description where it's crucial to engage the reader: in the (optional) tagline, in the opening lines, and in the ending lines.

A tagline is a hook, not a summary. It hints at the plot. Because a hint—the right hint—is all you need to snag a reader's attention.

Taglines are perhaps more commonly used to sell movies than books, because a movie poster has room for only a few words, if any, while book buyers may be willing to take the time to read several sentences or even several paragraphs to learn about the story.

Not every book has a tagline. Not every book *needs* a tagline. Nevertheless, a great tagline can certainly be a plus.

Because taglines are short, they often work in tandem with the cover image (or movie poster visuals) and/or with the title—meaning the tagline may not fully make sense on its own.

For example, the movie poster for the romantic comedy *Must Love Dogs* (directed by Gary David Goldberg). (Not a novel…so sorry. Based on the novel by Claire Cook, though.)

Its tagline?

The hardest trick is making them stay.

If all you knew was the tagline, you'd probably guess there's a commitment issue, but its nature would be unclear. Could the story be about an employer who's having trouble retaining employees? A rural town losing its young people to the big city? An artist who balances miniature angel figurines on the heads of pins?

Once you know the title and see the image of a woman and a man and a cute dog, it becomes clear the story is a romance or romantic comedy. The woman is smiling at the man, the man looks vaguely uncomfortable, and they're each sitting at opposite ends of a bench with the dog in the middle, so you figure the woman is having trouble finding a guy who's not commitment-phobic. It's not until this point that the play on words makes sense (commanding a dog to "stay"; convincing a romantic partner to commit).

In reality, the reader will see the cover image and the title first, so this uncertainty about what the tagline might mean will not arise. Instead, the reader will read the tagline and feel that sense of happy discovery and satisfaction that comes from watching all the pieces fit together and click into place.

The tagline doesn't *have* to tie in with the cover and the title, but at the very least, these elements shouldn't work against each other.

Here's another example:

This affair could *truly* last forever!

This tagline makes perfect sense on its own, with the word *affair* clearly indicating a romance. However, it takes on additional meaning when combined with the cover image—a couple embracing in the dark, a charm bracelet in the shape of a winged bat, the black and blood-red color scheme—and the title: *A Bite to Remember* (by Lynsay Sands). The vampire cues suggest their "forever" is no longer metaphorical but literal.

Word choice is important here. For example:

Lady + Duke = True Love?

(*Duke with Benefits* by Manda Collins)

The words *true love* signal a romance; the words *lady* and *duke* indicate a historical romance, likely Regency, which is reinforced by the beautiful period dress worn on the cover.

What's clever about this tagline is that it goes beyond word choice and takes the form of a mathematical equation, because the story features a heroine who is a mathematician—and for the mathematically minded, an equation communicates more effectively than sentences. If it had been any other plot, the arithmetic would have felt strange rather than perfectly delightful.

Above all, capture the reader's attention. The purpose of the tagline is to make the reader interested enough to want to (1) buy your book immediately, or (2) learn more about your book (and then buy it).

Ways to hook the reader include:

- an intriguing question
- a clear trope
- an unusual or surprising situation
- an unexpected twist

- compelling stakes
- conflict or danger
- humor
- a familiar expression, maxim, or play on words

An intriguing question

Mystery is not the central tenet of most romances, but if you can come up with a good question, it will draw the reader in. (See Chapter 8: *Supercharge the Ending* for more on this.)

Cinderella and Prince Charming...brought together by chance, or design?

(*Trust by Design* by Stacey Joy Netzel)

♥

What does a fiercely independent young widow really want? One determined suitor is about to find out...

(*The Earl Next Door* by Amelia Grey)

♥

How far would she go to become a mother?

(*My Convenient Marriage* by Rachel Taylor)

♥

She's in hot pursuit of The One, he's in hot pursuit of her. Can she see what's been in front of her all this time?

(*The Right Guy* by Kate O'Keeffe)

A clear trope

Superfans love their tropes. Get their attention quickly, and your work is done.

> She's getting married in ten days, but she doesn't remember the groom…
>
> (*Bride in Trouble* by Serenity Woods)

♥

> It's fake. But it feels so good.
>
> (*Mr. Fiancé* by Lauren Landish)

♥

> Enemies make the best lovers.
>
> (*Before Ben* by Cynthia Eden)

♥

> Never have I ever…fallen for my best friend.
>
> (*Blindsided* by Amy Daws)

An unusual or surprising situation

Familiarity can be comforting, but a new angle can be fun, too.

> Marrying a stranger to keep the woman's siblings out of an orphanage is one thing, but when more children than expected pour out of the stagecoach, what's a man to do?
>
> (*Tomorrow's First Light* by Naomi Rawlings)

♥

Lies can be the ties that bind...

(*To Love & Betray* by Shelly Ellis)

♥

Murder is a deadly way to start a relationship...

(*Taylor* by Dale Mayer)

♥

Remember that time you accidentally sexted your in-laws?

(*America's Geekheart* by Pippa Grant)

(Note the use of second-person POV, which I'll come back to in Chapter 9: *Traditional Structures*.)

An unexpected twist

To make this work, you'll need two parts (often phrased as two sentences)—first a setup and then a reversal of expectations. The resulting surprise captures readers' attention. Even (especially?) when the twist reveals a beloved trope.

Flynn hadn't expected to be getting married anytime soon. Definitely not this weekend. And definitely not to a man.

(*The Substitute* by Sean Ashcroft)

♥

I have a crush on my new neighbor. The one that

everyone hates.

(Crashed by Julie Kriss)

♥

She never wanted to be a superhero. Too much danger. Too much spandex…

(Jinx by Jennifer Estep)

♥

Your presence is requested at romantic Twill Castle for the wedding of Miss Clio Whitmore and…and…?

(Say Yes to the Marquess by Tessa Dare)

Compelling stakes

I'm not saying *high* stakes, because it took me a long time to understand how that term applied to romance novels. That's because it's usually described as life or death, and romance plots don't usually hinge on life-or-death situations. But that doesn't mean their stakes aren't meaningful. When the consequences of not getting what you want would be devastating, those are high stakes. The risk of an unhappy marriage, of losing love, or of losing a career can be just as compelling, and more relatable, than, say, the threat of planetary annihilation. (Although if that's your plot, go for it.)

When you spend your life at the top, there's only one direction you can go.

(Gold by E. J. Noyes)

♥

She's found the one—but he's already taken!

(*Accidentally Engaged* by Mary Carter)

♥

One-Night Stand Rule #1: Always check the condom's expiry date.

Oops.

(*Decidedly With Baby* by Stina Lindenblatt)

♥

She'd pushed him away—now her life depends on him coming back.

(*The Prime Objective* by Ginna Gray)

Conflict or danger

Many of the above examples could be described simply as conflict. Or you might think of it as danger: the characters are in danger of dying, getting in trouble, or simply not reaching their goals and getting what they want. Here are a few more examples that hint at impending danger:

It's only a little ruse...

(*An Agreeable Alliance* by Kasey Stockton)

♥

She's crashed the biggest party of her life, and she's about to pay the price.

(*Finding His Mark* by Brittney Sahin)

♥

What if your husband turns out to be the man sent to kill your ancestor?

(*Must Love More Kilts* by Angela Quarles)

♥

A lie brought them together. The truth could tear them apart.

(*Tru* by Bree Livingston)

Humor

Don't think your story's conflict is the main draw? Humor may be the way to go. Perhaps it's a humorous situation; perhaps it's a character's attitude toward a not-so-funny state of affairs. Even better, combine humor with conflict.

Pirate earl seeks wife. Squeamish ladies need not apply. Ability to treat gunshot wounds a plus.

(*Earl Interrupted* by Amanda Forester)

♥

"Are you calling dibs?"

"She's a woman, not the last piece of f**king pie. And yes, I'm calling dibs if it keeps your hands off of her."

(*No More Secrets* by Lucy Score)

(Note the use of dialogue, which I discuss in Chapter 11: *Dialogue and Excerpts*.)

♥

Okay, maybe hijacking an alien commander's warship wasn't her best idea...

(*Heart of Eon* by Anna Hackett)

A familiar expression, maxim, or play on words

Puns, plays on words, proverbs, maxims, idioms, familiar expressions, and twists on familiar turns of phrase can be fun. They're not necessarily a hook on their own, though. They work best if they incorporate one of the other elements mentioned above (a trope, a surprise twist, compelling stakes, conflict, humor, etc.).

Marry in haste, repent at leisure.

(*Not Quite a Wife* by Mary Jo Putney)

(a maxim...with compelling stakes)

♥

There's more than one way to lose your shirt...

(*Skintight* by Susan Andersen)

(a play on words...with compelling stakes)

♥

First comes love. Then comes...the most ill-timed proposal in history?

(*So Right* by Rebekah Weatherspoon)

(a twist on a children's rhyme...with conflict and a reversal of expectations)

♥

It's all fun and games…until someone falls in love.

(Daring Miss Danvers by Vivienne Lorret)

(a twist on a familiar expression…with humor)

♥

Relationships aren't rocket science. If they were, I might stand a chance of figuring one out.

(Rocket Science by K. M. Neuhold)

(an idiom…with conflict and a reversal of expectations)

♥

All's fair in love and war. Now they just have to decide which this is…

(Kilted Sin by Tammy Andresen)

(a maxim…with conflict and a trope)

One caveat: maxims and proverbs appeal because of their familiarity—and that's also their drawback. That last example's so popular it's made it into dozens of book titles, including *All's Fair in Love & Arson, All's Fair in Love and Cupcakes, All's Fair in Love and Debauchery, All's Fair in Love & Football, All's Fair in Love & Little League, All's Fair in Love and Road Rallies, All's Fair in Love & Seduction, All's Fair in Love and Weddings, All's Fair in Love and Wolf,* and *All's Fair in Love and Words.* (By, respectively, Sharon McGregor, Betsy St. Amant, Samantha Holt, Desean Rambo, J. J. Berducci, Diane M. Pratt, Beverley Kendall, Christine S. Feldman, Terry Spear, and Ann Herrick.)

Does the tagline have to be short?

Traditionally taglines have been extremely short because they had to fit on the cover of a paperback. Nowadays, that's not as much of an issue. As the earlier examples demonstrate, taglines don't have to be limited to a brief phrase.

Just keep in mind that you might encounter space limitations if you're producing a print version of the book, where you may not have room for a long tagline, especially if you want to set it in a large, fancy font.

On an online retailer's website, space for a longish tagline is obviously not an issue.

But attention spans are short. Encountering a four-sentence block of text or a complicated compound sentence is going to make some people's eyes glaze over. Be as spare and concise as you can.

And speaking of print books…

With paperbacks, the tagline usually appears on the front cover or at the top of the back cover. If you're overflowing with ideas and can't choose just one, you can even have two different taglines—one for the front and one for the back. For example:

When life gives you limes, make margaritas.

(*Sorry Not Sorry* by Sophie Ranald —
from the front cover)

♥

Charlotte has always been a good girl. But being good is getting boring…

(*Sorry Not Sorry* by Sophie Ranald —
from the back cover and the online description)

Then give it a rest and apply your creativity to writing the rest of the blurb.

LOGLINES

I began this chapter by saying a tagline is a hook, not a summary.

But-but-but…you've seen taglines that do summarize the whole story.

Yes. So have I.

I wouldn't call that a tagline, though. It's called a logline. A logline masquerading as a tagline.

A logline is a brief overview which condenses the entire plot into a single sentence (three at most) designed to be used in ads where space is limited or, for a movie or television show, in the viewers' guide. In just a few words, it identifies the characters, the main conflict, and the genre or trope. Perhaps even the setting. Kind of what the tagline does…without the coquetry.

Here are some examples:

A modern-day Muslim *Pride and Prejudice* for a new generation of love.

(*Ayesha at Last* by Uzma Jalaluddin)

♥

When fate throws a Confederate soldier and a Yankee heiress together, they'll uncover a fierce love worth fighting for...even if it means crossing enemy lines.

(*Surrender the Wind* by Elizabeth St. Michel)

♥

A closeted small-town florist and a too-busy-for-a-relationship bakery owner mix up the perfect recipe for love in this delicious lesbian romance novel.

(*Not the Marrying Kind* by Jae)

(Note the bakery-appropriate word choice of *mix*, *recipe*, and *delicious*.)

♥

Sparks fly when an accident-prone bounty hunter mistakenly apprehends the wrong guy.

(*Catastrophe Magnet* by J. B. Heller)

♥

He's a sea plane pilot determined to honor his convictions. She's a kayak guide who mocked his faith for sport. One small lakeside cabin in Alaska can't house them both.

(*Love Flies In* by Heidi McCahan)

♥

Torn from the twenty-first century, lost in the lonely Highlands of Scotland, a modern woman discovers the most important secret of all: that love transcends time.

(*Call of a Highlander* by Katy Baker)

If you want to use a logline to introduce your

description, go for it. It absolutely can work.

(And use it in your ad, too.)

In my opinion, this approach works best for stories that fall into a popular, well-known trope. This saves you from having to explain much of anything, as browsing customers can quickly identify the trope and immediately grasp whether they might be interested in your book. If they're a fan of that trope, you've got them.

If it's not a trope-based story, it's harder to entice a reader with a logline for two reasons: (1) there's not enough time to explain an unfamiliar story, and (2) summarizing gives a sense of completion, so the reader is satisfied and there's little urgency to keep reading.

Tagline (hints at the plot):

> Crash-landing on an uninhabited island with the boss was not in the job description.

Logline (summarizes the plot):

> When a CEO and her executive assistant survive a plane crash only to be stranded on an uninhabited island, they must work together to stay alive while navigating their growing feelings for each other...feelings the employee handbook doesn't allow.

In both versions, I indicate two tropes: stranded alone together and boss/assistant.

In the logline, I could have also mentioned the higher-level subgenre (contemporary romance) outright, which many authors do. This can help with discoverability (as I explained in Chapter 4: *Incorporate Keywords*), and if your logline is doubling as your brief ad, it makes even more sense to do this.

Just keep in mind that if the only reason you're naming the subgenre is for search engine optimization (SEO), it doesn't have to happen in the first line of your description, because search engines will find your target words no matter where they appear—beginning, middle, or end. You may prefer to reserve the prime location for human eyes—your very first lines—to tell the reader something he hasn't already deduced.

So how do you write a great logline? How do you summarize an entire novel in one sentence? Or even two or three sentences?

Step 1: Identify the characters, the conflict, and the subgenre or trope.

For example, I've seen authors do something like this:

> A vampire. The human who loves him. A paranormal romance.

Step 2: Don't panic.

The above is an example of an author who panicked. She knew she didn't have many words available, so she used the fewest possible words, and the result is bland—not necessarily because it's short, but because it's vague.

As I discussed in Chapter 5: *Be Specific*, detail is the solution.

Let's try to improve this.

(I'm going to stick with this commonly used *pow-pow-pow* ad-writer's voice, but remember you're not only selling your plot, you're also selling your writing style. Readers would rather get a sense of *your* voice than a voice you copied from other blurbs. Even when brevity is essential, you don't have to resort to two-word sentences to make your point.)

Let's start by adding a few specifics about this vampire and this human to sharpen our focus.

> A single dad. Who's a vampire. And the interfering first-grade teacher who just might win his heart.

Now we know two additional facts about each character (single dad, interfering first-grade teacher).

Also, in only a few words, I've mentioned (or at least alluded to) all three main characters (vampire, teacher, child) and three tropes (vampire, single dad, teacher/parent).

But it's still flat. If the reader loooves single-dad romances and/or loooves vampire romances, maybe this'll seem exciting. Otherwise…probably not.

Could that be because of the type of detail I included? What if I added details that are less external and more about feelings? Romance novels are, after all, about emotion, and that's what readers like about them.

> Peter never planned to be a single dad. Or a vampire. Or to fall for his daughter's interfering first-grade teacher. But love—and sudden night vision— aren't the sorts of things you schedule in your calendar.

Now we have a stronger emotional connection to Mr. I Didn't Plan Ahead For This, because we're given an emotional trait we can perhaps relate to.

Still kind of boring, though. Could that be because the

conflict is vague?

Yes. Yes it could.

Yeah, sure, the conflict is implied, because we can assume it's tough being a vampire and it's tough being a single dad, and who wants to deal with an "interfering" teacher? But we're filling in all those details ourselves, in our heads, and if we're skimming and not thinking too hard, the details aren't being filled in all that well.

How about if we spell it out?

> Getting his first-grader to school on time is a challenge for Peter now that he's single. And a vampire. And sunlight will kill him. If his daughter's teacher doesn't kill him first.

Now I've clarified three conflicts (living as a vampire among humans, struggling to manage a young child on his own, heated disagreements between teacher and parent) and an additional trope (enemies to lovers).

How did I sharpen the conflict? By focusing on small details such as Peter's difficulty getting his daughter to school on time and his fatal sun allergy. I listed obstacles, not just character traits.

I'm veering into tagline territory here, though, raising questions instead of summarizing. Guess I just can't help myself.

Okay, fine. I promised a logline, so I'll try again, this time replacing the external conflict (Will he live?) with the internal struggle (Can he love?) and wrapping it up. (I'm giving myself bonus points for reducing it to a single sentence.)

> Not every vampire has room in his unbeating heart for a family, but with a six-year-old daughter who needs him and the annoying first-grade teacher who clearly doesn't, this widower learns there are no limits on love.

Or, to stay true to the *pow-pow-pow* style we started with, I could pare it down to the essence of all romance novels: love wins.

> A vampire who's forgotten how to love. The six-year-old and the thirty-six-year-old who will make him remember.

"What is the story about?" is the question the logline must answer.

How to answer that question, and which details to include, are always judgment calls. The only way to really know is to run a poll or to test multiple versions and see which one sells better. Write and rewrite, and don't be afraid to scrap what you have and try a new approach.

7

OPTIMIZE THE OPENING

When you're browsing for books, do you spend more than two point five seconds reading blurbs? I don't. (Not until I hit one that intrigues me enough to consider buying.)

You need to get your readers' attention fast. Don't bore them. Don't confuse them. Catch their eye, engage their emotions, and say something so alluring they'll want to keep reading.

Every retailer limits the book description to a certain length, but a generous limit does not mean customers will see the whole thing. Websites prefer pictures to words. In a list of search results, if the book description appears at all, only a snippet is shown. Even on the product page—the page devoted solely to your book—many sites truncate the description and display only the first few lines. That can mean a mere one to three sentences, and if you start by introducing the series or how popular you are (*From* USA Today *bestselling author Rachel Writer comes her long-awaited return to Muskrat Creek with a stunning new saga of love and healing…*), you're left with even less.

How many readers click on "Read More" to reveal the full description? I'm guessing not many.

That means you're not just struggling against people's short attention spans. You're struggling against literal invisibility. People have to *take action* before they can see your full description, and that creates a roadblock that interferes with selling your book.

In general, online retail sites excel at encouraging sales by making it as easy as possible to compare products and their specifications. But not when it comes to books. Why? I have no idea. But rather than complain about things we can't change, the practical and sane thing to do is to do the best we can with the reality we're faced with. That means you must make your first lines count.

Even if you start with a tagline, treat the opening line of the main part of the description as if it's the first line people will see.

Consider this:

> American figure skater Carrie Parker's Winter Games dreams were dashed when her philandering partner caused one of the greatest scandals in skating history.
>
> (*Pairing Off* by Elizabeth Harmon)

Immediately we know quite a bit about who the main character is (she's an accomplished ice skater, she hoped to represent the U.S. at the Olympics, she didn't win a medal or perhaps wasn't able to compete), and our emotions are on alert (through no fault of her own, she failed to achieve her dream). We can also guess what she wants (she's presumably a pairs skater — confirmed by the image on the book cover and suggested by the title — so to continue to pursue her dream, she'll need a new skating partner), which sets up an additional conflict, revealed later in the blurb (the new pair will struggle to balance the demands of their sport with their feelings for each other). Another way to think about this is that we grasp the tropes (figure skating, Olympics, an athlete overcomes adversity).

The tropes, the protagonist, her goal, what's standing in her way...every one of these is a hook, and they're all packed into a mere 23 words. How amazing is that?

Note the necessary information about the character's identity is conveyed in the fewest possible words: American figure skater. With this technique, the protagonists are introduced not simply by name, but by preceding the name with a descriptive noun or an adjective/noun combination.

For example:

> Inventor Drake
> Perfectionist Drake
> Aspiring actor Drake
> Notorious pirate Drake
> Hopeless romantic Drake
> Jaded investigative reporter Drake
> Recent Guatemalan immigrant Drake
> Accident-prone high school robotics team captain Drake

This type of descriptor acts as a hook, because the reader knows what an inventor/pirate/immigrant is, while a random name means nothing to her.

Sometimes, for the sake of readability, it makes more sense to place the character's name first:

> Drake Dramatic, an aspiring actor desperate to land a role with the best director in Hollywood, has a full schedule of auditions lined up ... for toothpaste commercials.

Whether you use this method or not, try to position the most important details up front, where they'll be seen.

Consider this opening line I made up:

> Dr. Antoine Atwater owns a thriving medical practice in Atlanta with his younger brother, Leon, and his former brother-in-law, Raoul, but spends his summers birding in the swamp with his best friend.

Unless these brothers are integral to the plot, they're noise. They certainly don't belong in the prime selling position, a.k.a. the first sentence.

Yeah, I get it, you're mentioning them because this is a series, and Leon and Raoul are the heroes of the other books in the series, so they need to be there to explain how this book fits in with the others.

No.

You need to sell *this* book before you can hope to sell the entire series. Stick to the point of *this* book.

If you must explain that it's part of a series—and yes, I agree, you must—it's better to say so outright by placing that information in the metadata or the subtitle (*Doctors of a Feather: Book 1*). (I'll discuss series information in more depth in Chapter 12: *Extras*.)

If this is Book 3 in your series, and readers are going to buy it because they loved the first two books, and that's your main selling point, then the series may be important enough to highlight.

Just keep in mind that blathering on for an entire paragraph about the premise of the series is a good way to lose people's attention. Those lovely passages explaining the concept of the series used to work fine on a paperback, offset in a contrasting color, but an online product page provides a different visual landscape. Readers want to know about Antoine. If a wall of introductory words prevents them from seeing the good stuff, they won't feel compelled to click on "More" or the down arrow to see your hidden material. They'll feel frustrated, and they'll move on to another book.

So stay succinct. The book they've been waiting for is available now!

> The Doctors of a Feather are back, saving lives and breaking hearts.

Then forget about the distracting (and oh-so-hot) brothers and move on. Perhaps like this:

> Every summer, Dr. Antoine Atwater takes a break from saving cancer patients to wade through the swamp, hoping to spot endangered birds while he grieves for the patients he's lost.

Now the focus is on Antoine, where it belongs.

Notice I've also added a conflict: Antoine struggles with the emotional repercussions of his job. Instead of saying he co-owns a thriving business (doesn't everyone in Romancelandia?), I've made it more personal and more compelling by showing him in trouble (he can't save everyone, and he's not okay with that).

Conflict is crucial. Human beings are wired to pay attention to conflict, and it's the quickest way to forge an emotional connection with the reader. That's why a good opening not only identifies the character—and ideally the setting, the tone, and the subgenre—but also makes them interesting by highlighting a problem or conflict. This doesn't have to be the main story conflict; any obstacle or minor difficulty will do. Done well, not-so-serious conflict can be just as engaging as life-or-death peril.

Here are some examples that use various types of conflict in the opening lines:

> Like any good heroine, I have challenges to face. Getting my son to wear pants is one; dealing with my snooze-fest of a job is another.
>
> (*The Fix* by Sylvie Stewart)

(character, conflict, voice)

♥

> Holly Evans has just seen her own body laid to rest, and if it had been up to her, she wouldn't have chosen that particular polyester dress for the event.
>
> (*You Had Me at Halo* by Amanda Ashby)

(character, conflict, subgenre, voice)

♥

> Aspiring filmmaker and wallflower Twinkle Mehra has stories she wants to tell and universes she wants to explore, if only the world would listen.
>
> (*From Twinkle, with Love* by Sandhya Menon)

(character, conflict, voice)

♥

> One night. No one will know.
>
> (*Hate to Want You* by Alisha Rai)

(conflict, voice)

♥

After Brady Collins's ex-wife dies, he receives devastating news—his nine-month-old son Sam isn't his son at all. And Sam's wealthy maternal grandparents want custody of the child.

(*Honeysuckle Dreams* by Denise Hunter)

(character, conflict, voice)

♥

After a girls' night out, I expect to wake hungover—not next to a horned devil lovingly introducing himself as my husband. While he contemplates a name for our first child, refusing to leave my place, I call the cops.

(*Swipe Right for Husband* by V. K. Ludwig)

(character, conflict, subgenre, voice)

♥

Miss Miranda is not really a Miss, exactly. Nor is her name Miranda, exactly. But to escape her tyrannical duke of a father, changes were required.

(*Escaping His Grace* by Kristin Vayden)

(character, conflict, setting, subgenre, voice)

♥

Gillaine Davré is wondering where the last three hundred years have gone. Waking up in an unknown space station, the last thing the Special Forces captain remembers is her ship being attacked.

(*An Accidental Goddess* by Linnea Sinclair)

(character, conflict, setting, subgenre, voice)

♥

As the admissions director for one of Manhattan's finest private schools, Libby Kimmelman is overworked, underpaid—and totally overwhelmed by flowers, chocolates and other bribes from zealous parents determined to enroll their little Einsteins.

(*The Fixer Upper* by Judith Arnold)

(character, conflict, setting, voice)

♥

Wham, bam, no-thank-you, ma'am. That about sums up the sex life of Claire Doolittle.

(*Sleeping with Ward Cleaver* by Jenny Gardiner)

(character, conflict, voice)

Don't waste word count. Go straight to the conflict, and don't get sidetracked.

Then don't fizzle out afterward.

Each step of the process is a hook that leads to the next hook. If the tagline is compelling, the reader will move on to the opening. If they like the opening, they'll read the rest of the description. If the ending doesn't disappoint, they'll want to read the book.

8

SUPERCHARGE THE ENDING

People who mock the romance genre often say things like, "Why would you want to read romance? You already know how it ends!"

That's stupid.

Oops, sorry, didn't mean to be rude. I meant that's *uninformed*.

The fact that I, as a reader, already know the book ends in happily ever after does not constitute a spoiler nor take away from my enjoyment of the story one bit.

Do the romance-bashers say, "Why would you want to read mysteries? You already know how it ends! The sleuth solves the mystery!"

Do they say, "Why would you want to read thrillers? You already know how it ends! The good guys stop the bad guys!"

No?

As a romance reader, you already know there's more to the plot than the essential happily ever after, and as a blurb writer, you're going to touch on those other aspects of the plot. When you do, this is not the place to include spoilers or reveal plot twists. Present the conflict but not its resolution. Hint. Don't overshare.

A reader will buy your book because she wants to know more. (Or because she's in love with your characters.

More on that in a bit.) If you explain the whole plot and satisfy her curiosity, she no longer has a burning desire to read your book—and you've just killed a potential sale.

ENDING WITH A QUESTION MARK, ELLIPSIS, OR PERIOD

The desire to leave the reader hanging is why many book descriptions end in a question mark or an ellipsis (a.k.a. dot-dot-dot)—they're shortcuts that create a sense that things are unresolved.

Lots of taglines do this, too. It's the same idea. The tagline is trying to lure the potential buyer into reading more of the description. (*There's mooore... What could it beee...?*) The final line of the description is trying to entice the potential buyer to read the book itself.

Some people find question marks and ellipses annoying (some people find everything annoying), but here's why a question mark can work: The reader's brain is driving down the highway, forward, forward, forward, skim, skim, skim, go, go, go. When they encounter a question that makes them think, that pause reroutes them onto an off-ramp to a scenic detour. Their skimming is interrupted, their momentum slows, and information about your book starts to enter their thoughts and (we hope) stick around.

Unfortunately, with a romance, it can be almost impossible to find a question whose answer isn't obvious.

Will she learn to trust again?

Duh. Of course she will.

Will he allow himself to love?

Yes! Of course he will!

Will they end up together?

Ugh. No. That is *not* a real question.

And yet...

"Will they or won't they?" is *the* question in a romance novel, so it can feel maddeningly difficult, or even pointless, to end with any other question. And it's fine. It works. It's worth the effort to try out other possibilities, but if you do decide that "Will love win?" is what you want to end with, tailor it to your story and feel confident knowing you're in good company with lots of successful romance novelists.

Like these:

> Will they be able to overcome their pasts and find a love that lasts beyond one incredible summer?
>
> (*All Summer Long* by Susan Mallery)

♥

> Is Daniel really boyfriend material or is he maybe just a little too good to be true?
>
> (*The Boyfriend Project* by Farrah Rochon)

But back to punctuation. The truth is, question marks and ellipses are not needed to create suspense. They're not. At all.

Punctuation is the packaging, not the content. It's what's inside that counts.

Remember all the techniques that make a hook-y tagline or opening? They can be used again to create an attention-grabbing ending—especially a surprise twist, compelling stakes, or conflict. Danger, uncertainty, or tension—preferably, for romance readers, interpersonal tension—are what keep readers interested.

Once you've found your hook, any sentence can be reworded in a number of ways, so don't be afraid to try different versions and see which one is strongest.

Question mark: Will his secrets destroy their love?

Ellipsis: If his secrets come to light, their love may not survive…

Period: Love may be blind, but his secrets can't stay hidden forever.

Now on to some real-life examples.

Ending with a question mark

Should she return to her own time where her days are numbered? Or can she and Caleb find a love that stretches across time?

(*Her Place in Time* by Stephenia H. McGee)

(conflict, compelling stakes, uncertainty, subgenre)

♥

Could it be that the woman he captured is the only one who can touch the black heart he'd long thought dead?

(*The Highwayman* by Kerrigan Byrne)

(conflict, danger, compelling stakes)

♥

He needs to get Becca from "I won't" to "I do"…but how can he do that when she won't even say "I might"?

(I Do! by Rachel Gibson)

(conflict, compelling stakes, uncertainty)

Ending with an ellipsis

Now D must extract not one but *two* people from the most violent world he's ever encountered. And one of them is carrying his child…

(Midnight Revenge by Elle Kennedy)

(conflict, danger, compelling stakes)

♥

Soon it becomes unclear exactly who is seducing whom…

(Lessons in Seduction by Sara Bennett)

(sexual tension)

♥

There's a fine line between pretending to be in love and actually falling for your charming, handsome *fake* boyfriend…

(If I Never Met You by Mhairi McFarlane)

(conflict, sexual tension, trope)

Ending with a period

In one startling moment, the quiet life Grace has known is irrevocably altered, leaving her to question all she has been taught about love, family, and commitment.

(The Secret by Beverly Lewis)

(conflict, uncertainty)

♥

Her wedding has to be perfect, and perfect includes *not* having the baby halfway down the aisle.

(A Few Pecans Short of a Pie by Molly Harper)

(conflict, compelling stakes)

♥

Lilac and Tarver may find a way off this planet. But they won't be the same people who landed on it.

(These Broken Stars by Amie Kaufman and Meagan Spooner)

(conflict, danger, uncertainty, subgenre)

USING THE FINAL SENTENCE TO WORRY OR REASSURE

What I've neglected to mention until now is that, in romance novels, the final line of the description usually addresses the conflict in one of two ways:

1. Warning! It's going to be a train wreck.

Or...

2. Relax! Love will conquer all. The characters are going to change the collision course they're on and fall happily into each other's arms.

Note that your choice of the "train wreck" ending or the "they end up together" ending has nothing to do with the actual plot, because any plot can be described using either of these approaches.

Here's a relatively generic example:

Version 1 (train wreck):
As the election campaign heats up, it's hard to remember who's side she's on...

Version 2 (they end up together):
As the election campaign heats up, they can no longer deny that opposites attract...

In this one, I use a bit more detail:

Version 1 (train wreck):
Emily will do anything to save her school for orphans...even defy a vindictive duke.

Version 2 (they end up together):
Emily will do anything to save her school for orphans, because every orphan deserves a second chance...even, perhaps, a callous and very grown-up duke.

Why is the "they end up together" ending a valid option?

Everyone knows these two are going to end up

together, right? So why waste limited space reassuring your readers it all ends well, when you could leave them obsessed with wondering what happens next? Make them buy the book before they get to relax!

That's not how it works, though—not with romance.

For one thing, *because* everyone knows these two are going to fall in love and live happily ever after, calling the ending into question can seem disingenuous. (Eye rolling isn't the reaction we're going for.)

More importantly, when the "they end up together" ending is done well, it's not actually about everything turning out all right, but about the frisson of sexual attraction between the characters.

Romance readers read our books because they want to fall in love. Plot questions may make them curious, but ultimately, what they're really looking for is an emotional connection between the characters.

When an ending gives me that "awww, they're so cute together" feeling, it makes me want to read the book now-now-*now* because I can't wait to immerse myself in that experience.

That's a good reaction to have.

ECHOES

A great final sentence can be achieved with basic, serviceable writing. But add well-thought-out word choice, and you bring in a whole extra level of appeal.

I already discussed word choice (in Chapter 5: *Be Specific*), but I'm bringing it up again because the decisions you make when you're writing the ending really stand out.

This is your last chance to hook the reader, and it's all too easy to end on a weak note.

One way to give your ending a strong impact is to use the final line to echo the first sentence, the theme, the trope, or the book's title.

Sometimes this is done through outright repetition.

> When passions and ambitions overlap, Shelly and Claire must decide whether mixing business and pleasure can result in a perfect match.
>
> (*Unlikely Match* by Fiona Riley)

A perfect match repeats a word from the title and is a nice play on the setting (a matchmaking agency). Positioning the word *match* as the very last word leaves an echo in the reader's mind that circles her back to the title.

> Game on.
>
> (*Play* by Piper Lawson)

This story about a video game designer pairs two different but related words, ending with the word *game* to remind us of the word *play* in the title. This shows you don't have to repeat words verbatim to create an echo.

> Lottie and Ben are in for a honeymoon to remember, for better...or worse.
>
> (*Wedding Night* by Sophie Kinsella)

Again, *for better...or worse* evokes wedding vows and echoes the title without blatantly repeating the word *wedding.*

> **First line:** All through high school, I dreamed of kissing Nathan King.
>
> **Last lines:** But what if I fall in love with him? Again.
>
> (*Dear Future Ex-Wife* by Jillian Quinn)

Here, the first line introduces the trope (second-chance romance), and the last line emphasizes it. The author could have explicitly named the trope (*Will he give me a second chance?*), but instead found a single word (*Again.*) that says it all.

All the above examples use obvious echoes that the average reader skimming at high speed can't miss. That's not the only way to create this resonance, though. Here's an example where the echo is more subtle—and the echo isn't of the title or the trope, but of the characterization.

Quill Me Now by Jordan Castillo Price

> Spellcraft isn't exactly a respectable business, but it does pay the bills. At least, it *should*. Unfortunately, Dixon Penn failed his Spellcraft initiation. Instead of working in his family's shop, he's stuck delivering takeout orders in his uncle's beat-up Buick.
>
> Winning a Valentine's Day contest at the largest greeting card company in the tri-state area would be just the thing to get his life back on track—but something at Precious Greetings just doesn't add up. And despite numerous warnings to quit pestering them about his contest entry, he simply

> can't stop himself from coming back again and again.
>
> It doesn't hurt that the head of security is such a hottie. If Dixon had any common sense, he'd be scared of the big, mysterious, tattooed Russian.
>
> To be fair, no one ever accused him of being too smart...

In the first paragraph, we learn that Dixon failed his Spellcraft initiation. We may not know what a Spellcraft initiation is, exactly, but the fact that he failed it tells us he must be a poor student and/or a fuckup.

The final sentences (*If Dixon had any common sense,* and *To be fair, no one ever accused him of being too smart...*) fit perfectly with the motif that people think he's an idiot, and remind the reader of how the blurb began.

The author could instead have ended the description like this:

> It doesn't hurt that the head of security is such a hottie. But if Dixon allows himself to be distracted by the big, mysterious, tattooed Russian, he could be delivering burgers and cheese fries forever. Although it might be worth it...

Both versions imply the same thing: that a relationship with the Russian could cause problems for Dixon. In my version, by falling back on the default setting for romance novels—the characters' attraction to each other—I veer away from Dixon's unique personality and into Seen-It-Before-Ville. Instead, by keeping a firm handle on who the character is and choosing phrases consistent with that characterization, the author ensured all the pieces fit together and created something spectacular.

9

TRADITIONAL STRUCTURES

Now that you have your (optional) tagline, killer opening lines, and compelling ending, how do you put them all together and build a full description from here? How do you organize everything you want to say into a small amount of space?

Romance novels differ from most other genres in that they have more than one main character, so you potentially have a lot of ground to cover.

There are several traditional approaches to handling this:

- three-part/dual-protagonist structure
- two-part/dual-protagonist structure
- one-part/single-protagonist structure

THREE-PART/DUAL-PROTAGONIST STRUCTURE

The goal/motivation/conflict-based three-part/dual-protagonist structure is an extremely popular technique. The parts are broken down like this:

Section 1: The identity and situation (goal, motivation, and perhaps conflict) of the first protagonist of your choice (e.g., the heroine).

Section 2: The identity and situation (goal, motivation, and perhaps conflict) of the second protagonist (e.g., the hero).

Section 3: How the two protagonists intersect, connect, unite, and conflict. This includes a final line which relates to this conflict or this joining together. (Remember the "train wreck" versus the "they end up together" endings from Chapter 8: *Supercharge the Ending*?)

In other words:

Section 1: Who is this person? What does s(he) want? Why does s(he) want it? What's stopping him or her from getting it?

Section 2: Who is this other person? What does s(he) want? Why does s(he) want it? What's stopping him or her from getting it?

Section 3: These two individuals' goals are in opposition, so when their paths cross, there's conflict, because they can't both get what they want. Or the conflict is internal, and being around each other brings their issues to the surface. Or the protagonists join forces against a shared obstacle or enemy. (Or all three. Not that you have to include them all if that dilutes their impact.)

If Section 3 focuses on the conflict, you may not need to say anything about those obstacles in the first two sections. If it doesn't, the answer to "What's making things difficult?" should be given within each person's assigned section.

Which protagonist comes first? You could choose the main protagonist, if you feel there is one, but honestly, it doesn't matter. Try it both ways and see which version gives you the best flow.

The three sections are often, but not always, broken

into three paragraphs. The whole thing may be a single block of text, or it may be many, many paragraphs.

Here's an example:

Princess of the Sword by Lynn Kurland

- three-part/dual-protagonist structure
- "they end up together" ending

Section 1: Heroine

As the mercenary daughter of Gair, the black mage of Ceangail, Morgan is the only one who can stop the terrible sorcery her father unleashed. To do so, she must race against time and find the spell that will allow her to close the well of evil he opened. But that quest will lead her to places she never dreamed existed and into a darkness she would give anything to avoid...

Section 2: Hero

The fate of the kingdom of Neroche is intertwined with the closing of Gair's well. Miach, the archmage of Neroche, is determined to help Morgan find what she needs, not only because the safety of the Nine Kingdoms hangs in the balance, but also because he will do anything to protect her. Together they must search out the mysteries of Ceangail, and the dangers of Morgan's own bloodline.

Section 3: Both

Now, to rescue the kingdom from total ruin, Morgan and Miach have only each other to trust, heart and soul...

Let's break it down.

Section 1:

Who is Morgan? The daughter of a black mage.

What does she want? To find a spell—and use this spell to close a well of evil.

Why? Because she's the only one who can do it. It's implied she feels a responsibility to save the world.

What's stopping her? She's afraid, and she's racing against time. We can also guess that since her own father is the one who unleashed this evil, she'll likely feel conflicted about opposing him.

Section 2:

Who is Miach? An archmage.

What does he want? To help Morgan find this counter-spell, to protect Morgan on her quest, and to protect his kingdom from her father's evil spell.

Why? We can assume the survival of his kingdom's people is important to him. The world is at stake. And possibly he has romantic feelings for Morgan.

What's stopping him? Unclear. (Although we do learn there's danger lurking in Morgan's DNA.)

As you can see, Miach's section is more about his goal, while Morgan's section is more about her conflict. Totally fine.

Section 3:

We already know from Section 2 that Morgan and Miach will join forces, and that's reinforced here.

And ooh…they're going to fall in love.

HEADERS

A totally optional thing you can do with this structure is to use headers to delineate each section. They look amazing, especially on the back of a paperback, where they can be given a larger and more colorful contrasting font, so if you can come up with clever ones that capture the spirit of your book in a few words, go for it. If you can think of only one catchy header, and it makes sense as a hook for the whole story, you can use it at the top, at which point you'd call it a tagline. Or the reverse: if you have something in mind for the tagline that could be split into two or three parts, consider whether you'd rather use it as headers.

Better no headers than blah headers, though. If they're not hooking the reader or clarifying what's going on, they're clutter.

Headers can be used to identify who or what each section is about, or to stretch out the tagline so it's read in tandem with the blurb. Or both. The best headers are phrases that fit together to form a sentence and simultaneously relate to the sections they introduce.

The third section doesn't necessarily have to have a header. Here are two examples, one with and one without a third header:

An Earl Like You by Caroline Linden

- three-part/dual-protagonist structure
- two headers
- "train wreck" ending

Section 1: Hero

When you gamble at love…

When Hugh Deveraux discovers his newly inherited earldom is bankrupt, he sets about rebuilding the family fortune—in the gaming hells of London. But the most daring wager he takes isn't at cards. A wealthy tradesman makes a tantalizing offer: marry the man's spinster daughter and Hugh's debts will be paid and his fortune made. The only catch is that she must never know about their agreement…

Section 2: Heroine

You risk losing your heart…

Heiress Eliza Cross has given up hope of marriage until she meets the impossibly handsome Earl of Hastings, her father's new business partner. The earl is everything a gentleman should be, and is boldly attentive to her. It doesn't take long for Eliza to lose her heart and marry him.

Section 3: Both

But when Eliza discovers that there is more to the man she loves—and to her marriage—her trust is shattered. And it will take all of Hugh's power to prove that now his words of love are real…

♥

The Day of the Duchess by Sarah MacLean

- three-part/dual-protagonist structure

- three headers
- "they end up together" ending

Section 1: Hero

The one woman he will never forget…

Malcolm Bevingstoke, Duke of Haven, has lived the last three years in self-imposed solitude, paying the price for a mistake he can never reverse and a love he lost forever. The dukedom does not wait, however, and Haven requires an heir, which means he must find himself a wife by summer's end. There is only one problem—he already has one.

Section 2: Heroine

The one man she will never forgive…

After years in exile, Seraphina, Duchess of Haven, returns to London with a single goal—to reclaim the life she left and find happiness, unencumbered by the man who broke her heart. Haven offers her a deal: Sera can have her freedom, just as soon as she finds her replacement…which requires her to spend the summer in close quarters with the husband she does not want, but somehow cannot resist.

Section 3: Both

A love neither can deny…

The duke has a single summer to woo his wife and convince her that, despite their broken past, he can give her forever, making every day…the day of the duchess.

POINT OF VIEW (POV)

All of the previous examples are written in third-person point of view (he, she), but first-person POV (I) can also work in this format—all you need to do is mention the character's name to distinguish the first protagonist's section from the second protagonist's. The third section will also have to be from a single point of view (usually the second protagonist's, to avoid bouncing back and forth).

First-person narration has the feel of dialogue and can be a beautiful way to showcase your voice. (If your voice is not particularly interesting, you may be better off not trying this.)

The book itself does not have to be written in first person to use it in the book description, as long as the tone is a good fit. Nor does the POV of the body of the blurb have to match the POV of the tagline, which may be in first-, third-, or even second-person POV. (Refer back to Chapter 6: *Tantalize with a Tagline* for examples of all three.)

TWO-PART/DUAL-PROTAGONIST STRUCTURE

First-person point of view lends itself well to a modified version of the three-part/dual-protagonist structure I call the goal/motivation/conflict-based two-part/dual-protagonist structure. (Third-person POV also works.)

In this format, the third section is omitted, and the conflict and/or connection is included at the end of each protagonist's section.

Section 1: The identity and situation (goal, motivation, and conflict) of the first protagonist.

Section 2: The identity and situation (goal, motivation, and conflict) of the second protagonist.

Remember it's not about the number of paragraphs; it's about how the focus is distributed between the two protagonists. Whether the blurb is broken into two paragraphs or ten, with this approach you won't end with a final look at the two protagonists together.

It looks like this:

Strangely Amazing by Amiee Smith

- two-part/dual-protagonist structure
- first-person POV
- headers—because it's written in first person, the characters' names are used as headers to identify whose POV we're in
- transitional ending in the heroine's section and "train wreck" ending in the hero's section

Section 1: Heroine

Lilly Shepard

I check the box: geek. Gamer. Kinky. I don't have time for a relationship. I'm a scientist on a mission to eradicate disease. I don't have time for another wealthy man making lots of plans and promises. I have patients to heal. I don't have time for a handsome billionaire from Beverly Hills who is offering me a life people dream of... Well, maybe I can fit him in between a game of Grand Theft Auto and saving the world?

Section 2: Hero

Michael Ahmed

I'm ready to settle down and start a family. I want a wife. I think I've found her. But she's not impressed by my luxurious lifestyle or romantic gestures. She's not impressed by me. If only she could see that underneath my affluence is a guy who loves hip hop and R&B, home-cooked meals, and happily-ever-afters. Don't get it twisted, I'm an alpha male. I know what I want, and I don't stop until I get it. And I want her. But can I compete with her ambition?

Here's another example of the two-part/dual-protagonist structure, this one written in third-person POV:

How to Marry a Marquis by Julia Quinn

- two-part/dual-protagonist structure
- third-person POV
- headers
- "train wreck" ending in the heroine's section and "they end up together" ending in the hero's section

Section 1: Heroine

She's trying to follow the rules...

When Elizabeth Hotchkiss stumbles upon a copy of *How to Marry a Marquis* in her employer's library, she's convinced someone is playing a cruel joke. With three younger siblings to support, she knows she has to marry for money, but who might have guessed how desperate she's become? A guidebook to seduction might be just the thing she needs—and what harm could there be in taking a little peek?

Section 2: Hero

…But he's making his own

James Sidwell, the Marquis of Riverdale, has been summoned to rescue his aunt from a blackmailer, a task that requires him to pose as the new estate manager, and his primary suspect is his aunt's companion, Elizabeth. Intrigued by the alluring young woman with the curious little rulebook, he gallantly offers to help her find a husband…by practicing her wiles on him. But when practice becomes all too perfect, James decides that there is only one rule worth following—that Elizabeth marry her marquis.

ONE-PART/SINGLE-PROTAGONIST STRUCTURE

Do you have to follow the three- or two-part/dual-protagonist structure? Of course not. Although most romance novels do give both protagonists their due in the description (and it's a formula that should work for most romance plots), there's no need to follow this pattern. Non-romance novels do it all the time.

How? By using the one-part/single-protagonist structure, where the focus stays on a single character.

But-but-but…you have more than one protagonist.

Yup, if your book is a romance, you do. That doesn't mean you can't use this approach.

Think of it as "single point of view" rather than "single protagonist"—because what I mean by "single protagonist" is that we learn about the story from only one character's point of view.

Only one protagonist's situation (who is s(he), what does s(he) want, why does s(he) want it, what's stopping him or her from getting it?) is described. The love interest is mentioned, but we know very little about them and zilch about what they're feeling. Nevertheless, it's clear there's a romance.

Because this structure is more flexible than the others, it can be tempting to describe the plot as "This happens, then that happens, then *that* happens."

Try not to do that. Connect the dots so it's *because* this happens, then that happens.

Some situations require more "this then that" than others, but stay focused. No rambling. No tangents. No nonessential characters. No overexplaining.

It may help if, rather than thinking in terms of events, you think in terms of goal, motivation, and conflict, just as we did in the dual-protagonist structures. Or, at a minimum, goal and conflict.

Without a stated goal, any series of events will feel random. (She attends the ball! The duke rescues her from ruffians! Why? Uh…)

Without conflict, the blurb will be a snooze.

Motivation is sometimes omitted if the goal is easy to

relate to. (If she's trying to save her child's life, for example, there's no need to clarify the reasons why she'd do that.)

A blurb that has all three elements will be strongest.

Here are some examples:

Forecast by Jane Tara

- one-part/single-protagonist structure
- third-person POV
- ambiguous ending—it's not clear whether it's hinting at problems or promising happiness, which is a wonderful trick if you can pull it off

The Shakespeare women were what the locals of Greenwich Village called "gifted." Sure, Rowie's predictions were helpful for forecasting the weather or finding someone's lost grandkid. But when it came to love, her abilities were more like a curse. Why bother dating a guy if you knew at the first kiss he was destined for some blonde from New Jersey? Nope, Rowie was much happier bringing together the people she knew were a perfect match. Until the day she kissed the man whose future she couldn't foresee...

♥

A Lily in Disguise by Jessica Scarlett

- one-part/single-protagonist structure
- third-person POV
- "train wreck" ending

To escape the scandals tied to her name, Lillian Markley has gone by an alias for eight years. It was the only way for her to get a reputable job and save enough money to reunite with her sister in America. But when Lily is suddenly let go just as she's about to reach her goal, she's offered a salary she can't refuse in exchange for the unthinkable: She must masquerade as an heiress at a country estate for the summer.

Being exposed means facing prison, or worse— never seeing her sister again. Run-ins with kidnappers, a suspicious young boy, and a dangerous gentleman who knows her secret quickly have Lily spouting lies as often as she sips her tea—all while battling her growing feelings for Peter Wycliffe, the smiling host who seems to best her at every turn. Nothing is as simple as it seems. And as the falsehoods begin to mount, Lily must use her arsenal of wits to keep her three facades separate, while preventing Peter — and herself — from discovering the true woman beneath them all.

♥

Royal Tease by Nana Malone

- one-part/single-protagonist structure
- first-person POV
- "train wreck" ending

Once upon a time, I threw a princess over my shoulder and carried her out of a bar fight.

Jessa has carried that grudge ever since. Hates my

guts. She's uncooperative on her best days. Feisty. Stubborn. It's adorable. Not a word I'd ever tell my best friend, of course. Because she's his little sister.

The plan was royally simple. Go undercover and protect her. It should have been the easiest assignment of my life, but she is determined to cause trouble.

The stakes are too high to mess this up.

The monarchy is at risk.

And so is my heart.

HOW LONG SHOULD ALL THIS BE?

If you capture your reader's attention with your first sentence—and don't follow up by boring or confusing them—they should be willing to stick with you through to the end, however long the whole blurb is, so don't worry too much about keeping it super-duper short. But what qualifies as short? You want numbers!

If you plan to print a paperback edition, strive for 100 to 250 words; anything longer than that is not going to fit on the back cover. (It won't fit *attractively*. I'm sure you could use a tiny font and narrow margins and force your loquaciousness on there if you wanted to.)

For an ebook, you have the space to make it a lot longer, but most authors restrict the blurb to around 125 to 150 words. The more time and effort it takes to read your sales pitch, the more opportunity the reader has to lose interest and decide not to buy. Make it easy for them to give you a quick yes.

10

――――

ALTERNATE STRUCTURES

The point of the book description is to sell the book, not to follow a formula or to look a certain way. The point is to make the reader—the buyer—interested. Whatever it takes.

LISTS

Who says you have to describe the plot in complete sentences and formal, essay-like paragraphs? You don't!

Instead, you could borrow from the nonfiction playbook, with its beloved bullet points, and structure your description as a list.

Take the one-part/single-protagonist structure (who is s(he), what does s(he) want, why does s(he) want it, what's stopping him or her from getting it?), break free of your report-writing mindset, and see what happens.

Wildfire Griffin by Zoe Chant

When firefighter Rory lays eyes on fire watcher Edith, he instantly knows she's the one. His fated mate. Now, to win her heart, he just has to protect her from:

1. A raging wildfire. (*Actually, she's already got that covered, thanks.*)

2. The lightning-throwing invisible monster that started it. (*Um, the what?*)

3. Killer bunnies. *(Don't even ask.)*

4. The appalling matchmaking attempts from his crew of misfit shifters. (*Not only is this guy scorching hot, his dog is adorable too. And…weirdly smart?*)

5. His own animal need to claim her. Now. *(If only she could look him in the eye…)*

Good thing that as a powerful griffin shifter, he can handle anything…right?

There's only one problem.

The last thing this autistic woman wants—or needs—is to be protected…

Plot, conflict, personalities, voice… It's all here.

In this case, the blurb flows seamlessly from the introduction to the list to the ending.

Now here's another list that's purely a list, plus an explanatory header—this time in the form of step-by-step instructions written in the style of a self-help article.

The Honeymoon Trap by Christina Hovland

How to Survive Your Next Relationship Disaster 101

Step 1: Get pumped. Your new house, in your new town, comes with a sexy and shirtless man next door. Score!

Step 2: Don't let your freak-out show when Mr. OMG Shirtless turns around—and it's your old crush.

Step 3: Hold your head high when you run into him again on the first day of your new job—literally—and spill coffee all over yourself.

Step 4: Stay calm when he introduces himself as your new boss…and then announces that your first assignment is to go on a fake honeymoon together.

Step 5: Keep your $h*t locked tight when the new boss/old crush and you are forced to sleep in the same room…with one bed.

Step 6: Try to ignore just how freaking hot he is, and how much you want to touch him…

Both these examples are numbered lists of obstacles or conflicts. But a list can take many forms. Other possibilities include a to-do list, a bucket list, a pros-and-cons list, a multiple-choice quiz, a shopping list, driving directions… perhaps I'm getting carried away.

The format should be a natural extension of your story, though.

I'd only use a multiple-choice quiz, for example, for a contemporary teen romance set in a classroom, or perhaps a story involving a game show. Using a quiz to describe a historical romance set in a time period before multiple-choice quizzes were commonplace? Sure, some readers will be charmed. But curmudgeons like me? We'll shake our heads at your anachronistic whimsy and buy someone else's book.

Writing is always about making choices. If you decide to try an offbeat technique, don't do it because you think it's cute or clever or popular. Do it because it fits your story.

FREEFORM STRUCTURE

There are lots of other ways to blurb your book that break free of the traditional format. What I call freeform structure goes beyond the typical look and gets creative. A blurb like this relies on its strong personality to charm the reader into not noticing all the specifics he isn't being told.

Here's one example: the fake dictionary definition.

Mad About the Duke by Elizabeth Boyle

Madness \'mad-nes\ n (14c): the quality or state of being mad: a: rage b: insanity c: extreme folly d: ecstasy, enthusiasm.

And, added in the margins of the dictionary owned by James Tremont, the 9th Duke of Parkerton, one additional definition:

e: the state of finding oneself mistaken for a solicitor by a duke-hunting beauty who needs to be enthusiastically taught the true meaning of love.

Rage, insanity, extreme folly, and ecstasy will most likely be involved.

This example demonstrates just how little needs to be said about the plot or the characters. It says almost nothing about who the protagonists are. (The ninth Duke of Parkerton and a beautiful woman.) It says very little about what they want. (She wants to marry a duke, but what *he* wants (aside from wanting *her*) is anyone's guess.) The conflict is vague. (A case of mistaken identity?) And yet, at least in my opinion, it works. It shows that explaining everything is not the key to intriguing the reader.

This next one is a variant of the dictionary definition, but because the protagonist is a librarian, the description fittingly takes the form of a library card catalog entry, complete with a library call number and fake subject headings. You have to see the paperback edition to appreciate the full effect: the text is arranged to look like one of those rectangular cards that were stored in endless tiny drawers in card catalog cabinets in the days before everything was digitized.

This time there's lots of detail about the plot, but the characters remain vague.

The Librarian and the Spy by Susan Mann

327.1   SPIES, falling in love with, becoming

A librarian's journey from the checkout desk to fast cars, stolen treasures, and international intrigue / with an introduction by suave, handsome "insurance" agent James Lockwood.

Adventure-hungry Quinn Ellington's job solving mundane mysteries for library patrons entangles her in a mission to decode the whereabouts of a weapons cache from a priceless work of art before arms dealers beat her to it. Her adventure is filled with twists, turns, and a budding romance. Transcontinental pursuit, daring rescues, and intense covert flirting follow.

1. Spies—attractive. 2. London—criminal networks. 3. London—Harry Potter references. 4. Libraries—secrets of. 5. Best friends—nosy. I. Ellington, Quinn.

This next example does the reverse, saying very little about the plot while bringing the protagonist vividly to life. It's styled as a competition entry form.

Tourist Trap by Emma Harrison

LOGAN LAKE COUNTY FAIR

ENTRY NAME: Cassandra Grace

EVENT: Horseback riding (jumping)

ANIMAL NAME: Lola (best horse in the world!)

FEE ENCLOSED: Um, almost...

See, the thing is, I almost have enough money, I have tons of riding students who pay me, but there's this guy, and every time he calls I have to see him, so I've kind of been skipping work lately...but I'll have the fee soon, I promise!

Other possibilities for outside-the-box formats include:

dating profile
diary entry
employment ad
recipe
vacation rental home listing
wedding invitation

Or perhaps a book club Q&A:

The Billionaire Book Club by Max Monroe

The Billionaire Book Club Questionnaire

#1: Who is your least favorite character in the book?

Me—Caplin Hawkins. I am an absolute idiot.

#2: Who is your favorite character?

Gorgeous, addictive, insanely challenging Ruby. She's smart, driven, self-confident, and so beautiful, she makes my chest ache.

#3: What is your biggest takeaway from the story?

Ruby Rockford and I are meant to be. I just have to prove it to her.

Or a letter:

The Last Letter by Rebecca Yarros

Beckett,

If you're reading this, well, you know the last-letter drill. You made it. I didn't. Get off the guilt train, because I know if there was any chance you could have saved me, you would have.

I need one thing from you: get out of the army and get to Telluride.

My little sister Ella's raising the twins alone. She's too independent and won't accept help easily, but she has lost our grandmother, our parents, and now me. It's too much for anyone to endure. It's not fair.

And here's the kicker: there's something else you don't know that's tearing her family apart. She's going to need help.

So if I'm gone, that means I can't be there for Ella. I can't help them through this. But you can. So I'm begging you, as my best friend, go take care of my sister, my family.

Please don't make her go through it alone.

Ryan

Again, any novelty format runs the risk of seeming gimmicky, so it's best to use it only if it relates in some way to the actual story. Otherwise, you're misleading the reader into expecting a different kind of book than they're going to get.

11

DIALOGUE AND EXCERPTS

After seeing all these formats, it should be clear there is no one right way to write a book description.

Remember this if you choose to use dialogue in your description, because some people hate it.

To me, dialogue is nothing more than an excerpt, even if it's only one line. And an excerpt, in theory, is the ultimate showcase for your writing. Which should be a good thing, right?

The problem with a single line of dialogue, however, is that it's stripped of its context, and without context, the best line in the world loses its power. Worse, it could be confusing.

So proceed at your own risk.

In Chapter 6: *Tantalize with a Tagline*, one of the examples used a line of dialogue as the tagline. Here's another example:

> "Be careful, Amelia—you know how reckless you can be!" —Mrs. Charlotte Harris, headmistress
>
> (*Never Seduce a Scoundrel* by Sabrina Jeffries)

In my opinion, this one works, because combined with the title and the cover (the classic clinch), it manages to convey several hooks: it's clear this is a historical romance, it's clear this is the innocent-young-woman-who-craves-adventure-in-a-restrictive-society-(and-finds-it-with-a-man) trope, and there's definitely conflict.

A more dangerous way to incorporate dialogue is to use it as headers in the two- or three-part/dual-protagonist structure to introduce each character's section.

Here's a made-up example of what I mean:

"I never told my boyfriend I was pregnant."

Suzy has everything under control. Being a single mother isn't easy, but at least she made absolutely sure she'd never have to fight over custody with that snake.

"I like you, but I'm hung up on someone else."

Five years and thousands of frequent flyer miles later, Joshua can't forget the brilliant engineer he accidentally betrayed. He wishes he could, because it's interfering with his love life. It's not productive to compare every woman he meets to someone who will never take him back.

Does this dialogue showcase my voice? No. Is it interesting? No.

And who are these characters talking to? Uh…

Okay, so maybe your dialogue is better than this.

But if it's repeating information that's evident from the rest of the description, as mine is in this example, then it's a waste of space. Sorry. If you can do away with it and not lose anything, think about deleting it.

If you're not sure? Delete it.

Really.

But-but-but…readers like dialogue! They see blocks of text and flinch and avert their eyes. Break things up with dialogue, and they'll keep reading. Won't they?

Not necessarily.

When dialogue works, it works because it's immediate, it's engaging, and it draws the reader in.

But this will only happen if you choose the right excerpt. The quotation marks aren't magic. What's *inside* the quotation marks is what holds the reader's interest. A mundane comment will not be transformed into an appealing hook just by turning it into a quote.

If your characters are prone to saying outrageous things, then sure, go ahead and quote something shocking.

> "Friends with benefits, stepbrother with benefits, what's the difference?"
>
> (*Stepbrother with Benefits 1* by Mia Clark)

Just keep in mind that whatever its shock value or beauty or hilarity, or how much it gives a taste of your writing style, dialogue must be easily understood without any background information, especially if it's used as the opening line. The best excerpt will also convey basic information about the plot, such as the subgenre or conflict.

How about using several lines of dialogue? Will that fix the lack-of-context problem?

Maybe.

Maybe not.

In the following example, the description begins with an excerpt (consisting almost exclusively of dialogue) before launching into a more traditional description of the plot.

Getting Over It by Anna Maxted

"Maybe it will be good for you to be on your own for a bit."

"Why?" I say in a bored tone.

Lizzy dabs her mouth with her napkin (her perfect lipstick remains perfect) and declares, "You've got to be happy alone before you can be happy with someone."

"Liz," I say, "did you read that in *GirlTime*?"

"I might have," says Lizzy airily. "So?"

"I wrote it."

Wickedly funny and unfailingly honest, *Getting Over It* charts the misadventures of Helen Bradshaw, a caustically charming twenty-something who isn't exactly living out her dreams. [...]

Even if the reader never reads the full description, she'll have formed a mental picture of what to expect from this book.

The first two lines on their own would have been too unmoored to be interesting, but as part of the longer excerpt, there's just enough information that the dialogue—and the punch line—make sense.

Is it significant that only the hardcover edition of this book used the excerpt? Hmm...

Although the digital and print versions of the description are usually identical, excerpts are the exception.

Whatever the reason, the fact is that excerpts are more commonly seen in print books than in digital. I think it's because there's more space available to accommodate an excerpt in a physical book than there is online on a bookseller's website with restrictive display fields. A hardcover, which typically will print rave reviews and endorsements from famous authors (the other, more traditional meaning of *blurb*) on the back of the dust jacket, can instead print an excerpt on the back and still have plenty of room on the inside jacket flap for both the book description and the author bio. A paperback can print the book description on the back and reserve the interior's first page for a juicy excerpt too long or too risqué for the cover.

That doesn't mean you can't include an excerpt in the online retailer's book description field, but it'll have to be really short and really good, and it means you'll have less space remaining for your actual description.

Or, on Amazon, in countries where Author Central is available, you can log in there and place the excerpt on your product page in the fields called "From the Author", "From the Inside Flap", or "From the Back Cover".

12

EXTRAS

In addition to the main description, there are some extras you may want to add—or avoid—at the end:

- series information
- HEA/HFN notice
- genre, heat level, novel length
- trigger warning / content note
- joke trigger warning
- author biography
- comparable authors
- reviews, endorsements, accolades, awards

SERIES INFORMATION

The reader should be able to tell at a glance whether a book is part of a series. Most online retailers allow authors to indicate this in the metadata (it's one of those fields you fill out when you upload your book to the site), so *Book 2 of 5: The Jeweler's Daughters* will be clearly listed below the title or elsewhere on the product page. Series information may also be indicated within the title itself, as a subtitle (*Sapphire Sky: The Jeweler's Daughters, Book 2*), on the book's cover image, or in the description (*In the eagerly anticipated follow-up to* Garnet Sunrise, *Ashley Author returns to Crystal Bay with a heartwarming addition to The Jeweler's Daughters series that proves it's never too late for love.*) Or all three.

For series that aren't clearly numbered, or even those that are, you may want to include a list at the end of the description providing the recommended reading order.

Like this:

> Each book in The Jeweler's Daughters series is a standalone and can be enjoyed out of order. However, the recommended reading order is:
>
> 1: *Garnet Sunrise*
> 2: *Sapphire Sky*
> 3: *Opal Moon*
> 4: *Emerald Waters*
> 5: *Amethyst Nights*

As I did in this example, it can be helpful to mention whether each book is a standalone or not, as a series can consist of either loosely connected standalones or tightly interconnected books that are essentially one long story and must all be read in sequence before the couple rides off into the sunset. Some series even include both types— for example, a number of standalones interspersed with a few novellas that are not meant to be read separately. You wouldn't want a new reader to shy away from starting at fan-favorite Book 5 and lose you a sale if it's not necessary.

Another way to prevent that reader from hesitating is to combine this information with an assurance that the characters end up happily together and in love. You know…HEA.

HEA (HAPPILY EVER AFTER) /
HFN (HAPPY FOR NOW) NOTICE

I don't know when it happened or why, but at some point someone started the trend of ending the book description with what I call the HEA/HFN notice.

> This standalone romance has an HEA and no cliffhangers.

Or…

> No cheating, no cliffhangers, and a guaranteed happily ever after.

When I read this in a blurb, I feel like I'm being treated like a child. I should be able to tell from the description that it's a romance, and personally, I've never come across a book that was marketed as a romance and did not end happily.

(Okay, *once*. And it was literary fiction.)

(Plus that heartbreaking, bittersweet one where the heroine died at the end.)

(And the one that was the start of a series and unexpectedly just stopped without anything being resolved…)

(Okay, fine. It happens. I still say it's irritating.)

But maybe that's just me.

If you like it? Go for it. I guess.

GENRE, HEAT LEVEL, NOVEL LENGTH

This sweet romantic comedy is 80,000 words.

Genre

Noting the genre, subgenre, or trope may be restating the obvious, but some people like to do it. (I explained why in Chapter 4: *Incorporate Keywords* and Chapter 6: *Tantalize with a Tagline*.)

That does not mean this is an opportunity to list your keywords. You can dress them up to look like a sentence, but you are fooling no one. Yes, I am a huge fan of keywords, but I'm an even bigger fan of showcasing your writing style, and awkward attempts at keyword stuffing make authors look like bad writers. If it looks like this, it's not exactly stellar prose:

> Perfect for fans of billionaire romance, ugly duckling, Cinderella, rags to riches, contemporary romance, set in Shanghai.

No thanks.

Keywords have an assigned field. Use it.

Okay, then how about bulleted lists?

♥ workplace romance
♥ overly caffeinated coworkers
♥ so many spreadsheets
♥ an interfering kangaroo
♥ a thousand reasons not to fall in love
♥ a swoon-worthy HEA

(What did I do at the end there? An HEA! Nooo...)

This type of list is an attractive solution to the readability problem, but you do run the risk of getting in trouble (and honestly, why have rules if they're not going to enforce them? Until they do? Unpredictably?) for violating the no-lists-of-keywords-in-the-book-description-field rule. This shouldn't be an issue if your list is more cutesy than searchable (as in the example above), in which case, go right ahead.

Heat level

Noting the heat level pinpoints an aspect of genre that's difficult to clarify in the book description yet essential for readers to know.

It's so difficult to identify the sensuality level organically through the description that it's usually communicated by the book cover instead—stereotypically with a scantily clad torso or a pretty cottage garden.

It doesn't help that we're saddled with code words like *steamy* or *spicy* or *sweet*, because not every reader is familiar with these terms (the meaning of *sweet*, in particular, is not intuitive, which is no doubt what led to the use of the problematic but easier-to-understand *clean*), and those who *are* don't always agree on the nuances.

The words aren't ideal, but until we adopt a number-based system, as some book reviewers do, ranking books on a scale of one to three flames or one to five hot peppers, words are what we have. For a romance that's extremely hot or extremely not, it may be worth making an effort.

Word count

Although the page count (real or estimated) is always displayed elsewhere on the product page (occasionally word count is as well), some authors like to include the word count in the description field, where it's more easily noticed. Experienced ebook readers will understand that 30,000 words is a novella and 150,000 words is a commitment, and will be grateful to have that information at hand, likely while noting the price. Other readers will have no idea how word count translates into length. That means listing the word count says something about which audience you're targeting—and who you're willing to alienate with writerly jargon. It also marks you as an indie, since traditional publishers never include the word or page count when describing what their books are about—they think like cataloguers and restrict that information to its designated field.

TRIGGER WARNING / CONTENT NOTE

Note: This novel depicts violence that may be disturbing to some readers.

We're used to seeing warnings about extreme violence, nudity, and language in movies and television. Now we're also seeing these warnings on books.

Love them or scoff at them, trigger or content warnings—which flag emotionally difficult material—are not only a courtesy extended to the public but also a way to avoid poor reviews from angry readers. If the description itself doesn't bring the potentially upsetting topic to light—which is a more organic approach, if you can avoid spoilers—and you're not writing in a subgenre where knowing the subgenre is warning enough—you may want to consider spelling it out in an extra line at the end of your description. (Tailored to the medium, of course. Because nudity? In words? Let's be real.)

Some people feel the warning must specify precisely what the issue is, if it is to be useful, while others feel it is best to not name the potential trigger on the product page, as the warning itself could be traumatizing, but to instead direct the reader to another location where more information can be found—such as the author's website or the front matter of the book itself, if this can be previewed before buying.

Then there's the reverse trigger warning.

Remember *No cheating, no cliffhangers, and a guaranteed happily ever after*? "No cheating" may make *me* roll my eyes, but for some, it reassures the reader she is safe from this unfortunate turn of events. Even the HEA notice itself is kind of a reverse trigger warning as well.

Successful marketing means successfully targeting your audience. This is just one more way to help people avoid your book if they're going to hate it.

JOKE TRIGGER WARNING

Warning: This science fiction romance features a nerdy pilot, an even nerdier astrophysicist moonlighting as a pole dancer, and sexy aliens who engage in gunfights, snark, and repeated violations of the laws of physics.

I used to enjoy these "warnings" and admired them as an easy way to shoehorn keywords into the description. But now that I've given it more thought, I've come to realize the format belittles true trigger warnings.

Using the word "Warning!" may seem funny, but those who take content warnings seriously will not be amused. Whether an actual potential trigger is named or not, you can accomplish the same thing without framing it as a joke.

AUTHOR BIOGRAPHY

Imagine you've captured a reader's attention, and they've read to the end of the book description, and it's time to decide whether to buy. And now, within the description box, they encounter your biography. Will learning a little about you, the author, make a difference?

If the reader is someone who thinks, *Ugh, I never read the bio, let's skip this*, you've just inserted a negative experience that may break the spell you've woven and possibly push them away.

If the reader *is* interested in who you are? Will this interjection make them want to buy the book *more*?

I doubt it.

When you write nonfiction, readers are likely to be interested in what your qualifications are and why you're an expert, because it helps them trust that you know what you're talking about. When you write fiction, qualifications don't mean much. (Unless it's your appearance on a bestseller list. That might count. Your college degree and your entertaining labradoodle? No.)

Besides, many retailers have a dedicated area where you can type in your bio. I'd put it there, not in the book description field.

On sites where there is no "About the Author" field, then okay, if you insist, this is where you have to put it.

To be clear: I'm not saying you shouldn't share fun facts about yourself (and your hobbies/marriage/ children/pets); your personality *can* sell books. Or so I hear. I'm saying you can showcase your personality elsewhere.

COMPARABLE AUTHORS

If you like Francine Famous, you'll love this poignant journey through time to medieval Bruges.

Some authors lack confidence in their blurb's ability to fully convey their novel's tone, style, or awesomeness, so, as a form of shorthand, they compare their work to that of a bestselling author. If you go this route, be sure to choose an author whose work really is like yours. She must be a recognizable name so readers don't think, *Huh? Who?*, yet not so successful they'll pity you for being delusional. It's a tough—perhaps impossible—balance to find.

REVIEWS, ENDORSEMENTS, ACCOLADES, AWARDS

Imagine—again—you've captured a reader's attention with your book cover, and now they're salivating to read what the book's about, and the first thing they encounter within the description box is a flood of one-line excerpts from glowing reviews.

Or they've read to the end of the book description, and it's time for them to decide whether to buy, and the screen is filled with boldfaced, exclamation-pointed accolades.

You know, these:

> "A beautiful inspirational romance." — *Faith is the Word Book Reviews*

> "A heartwarming story of faith, hope, and devotion. I wish I'd written this!" — *Big-Name Author*

Will these make a difference?

Possibly.

Reviews are of course a good thing, and help sell books. They're a form of social proof, which is an essential way to build trust with a customer buying a product he can't touch from a person he doesn't know. Placing reviews in the book description field means you get to choose the ones you like, highlight your favorite parts, and make sure readers see them first—before they get to the site's other reviews (the ones you have no control over).

Awards, too, show that someone else liked your book. Readers who respect the award and value the opinion of judges who are held to a higher standard than the anonymous public may be convinced to buy, although you run the risk that others may be scared off if they believe awards are elitist and don't reflect their taste.

Endorsements from well-known authors—yet another form of social proof—might be helpful (traditional publishers certainly seem to think so), and if you're lucky enough to have them, of course you want to show them off.

Reviews, awards, endorsements, praise, praise, praise… Personally, I get annoyed by all that clutter on the screen making it harder for me to find the actual description. My eyes are tired. I'm impatient. I skip it.

I am not the only one who does this.

Then again, some readers need it. They need to know someone else recommends the book before they'll take a chance on it themselves.

Unfortunately, on most retailers' sites, the book description field is the only way for you to get those curated reviews onto the product page.

Fortunately, Amazon does have a dedicated area where you, the publisher (through Author Central, in countries where it's available), can post editorial reviews (meaning the reviews were written by professional reviewers or bloggers). It's less prominently displayed farther down the screen, and it's not as obvious an area for readers to glance at, but it's appropriate.

And, despite all evidence to the contrary, placing reviews, quotes, or testimonials in the description field is a violation of Amazon's guidelines.

Another option is to use the book cover itself to highlight an endorsement or award.

13

DO YOUR OWN RESEARCH

Just as different readers enjoy different books, and you may hate a book your best friend loves, different readers will be drawn to different blurbs. You may have read some of the examples in this book and hated them.

That's okay.

If you disagree with me (and even if you agree!), do your own research. Browse your own book collection, visit the library or bookstore, or scan the bestseller lists for your category. Look especially at books in your own subgenre.

It may seem logical to focus on the best-known mega-successes, but often that's not the ideal place to look. Why? Because big-name authors can get away with bad blurbs. That doesn't mean their blurbs *are* bad. (In fact, I quote many bestsellers in this book.) But is the blurb what's selling the book? Not necessarily. Readers have those authors on auto-buy. Lots of fans will never even look at the description, or will buy *despite* the description, because they love that author and are convinced they'll love everything that author writes. Those books are selling primarily because of the author's name.

It's the names you've never heard of who show up on the bestseller lists who are likely to be doing something really right in their book description (and with their title and cover design).

So look around. Find what you like. Figure out what it is you like about those descriptions. Then write your own.

And always remember that times change.

It used to be considered clever business practice to name your company something that started with the letter *A* so it would be listed first alphabetically in the yellow pages, because it was common knowledge that potential customers would turn to that section of the phonebook and call the first company listed.

This gave rise to a slew of businesses named AA Heating and Cooling, Aadvantage Appliance Repair, AAAA Plumbing, etc.

Now that paper phonebooks are collecting dust and online listings tend to be sorted by relevance and other factors rather than alphabetically, that trick is likely not helping those companies attract new customers anymore.

So maybe think twice before falling in love with the latest gimmick or advice on how to get more sales—including mine.

No one knows the secret to succeeding in this business, so we authors guess. And experiment. And start rumors that get passed on and repeated until they become enshrined as gospel.

Listen to the rumors and the advice, but test them out and decide for yourself.

YOU CAN DO IT!

During the course of my own research for this book, I came across many uninspiring blurbs for books that may well be wonderful reads, and it made me sad to think those books might never find their audience.

I also found many beautiful, moving, funny, unexpected, and intriguing book descriptions that left me in awe. Discovering them made me fall in love with the romance genre all over again.

I hope one day soon *your* next big fan will discover *your* book, and read the blurb, and find it irresistible.

BIBLIOGRAPHY

Note: The book description or cover copy quoted in this book may differ from the version in current use.

Andersen, Susan. *Skintight*. Copyright © 2005 by Susan Andersen. Published by MIRA Books, an imprint of Harlequin Enterprises.

Andresen, Tammy. *Kilted Sin*. Copyright © 2019 by Tammy Andresen. Independently published.

Arnold, Judith. *The Fixer Upper*. Copyright © 2005 by Barbara Keiler. Published by MIRA Books, an imprint of Harlequin Enterprises.

Ashby, Amanda. *You Had Me at Halo*. Copyright © 2007 by Amanda Ashby. Published by New American Library, a division of Penguin Group (USA) Inc.

Ashcroft, Sean. *The Substitute*. Copyright © 2018 by Sean Ashcroft. Independently published.

Ayres, D. D. *Rival Forces*. Copyright © 2016 by D. D. Ayres. Published by St. Martin's Paperbacks, an imprint of St. Martin's Press.

Baker, Katy. *Call of a Highlander*. Copyright © 2019 by Katy Baker. Independently published.

Bennett, Sara. *Lessons in Seduction*. Copyright © 2005 by Sara Bennett. Published by Avon Books, an imprint of HarperCollins Publishers.

Betts, Heidi. *Loves Me, Loves Me Knot*. Copyright © 2009 by Heidi Betts. Published by St. Martin's Paperbacks, an imprint of St. Martin's Press.

Bowen, Sarina. *Overnight Sensation*. Copyright © 2019 by Sarina Bowen. Published by Tuxbury Publishing.

Boyle, Elizabeth. *Mad About the Duke*. Copyright © 2010 by Elizabeth Boyle. Published by Avon Books, an imprint of HarperCollins Publishers.

Byrne, Kerrigan. *The Highwayman*. Copyright © 2015 by Kerrigan Byrne. Published by St. Martin's Paperbacks, an imprint of St. Martin's Press.

Caldwell, Siri. *Mistletoe Mishap*. Copyright © 2017 by Siri Caldwell. Published by Brussels Sprout Press.

Carter, Mary. *Accidentally Engaged*. Copyright © 2007 by Mary Carter. Published by Kensington Books, an imprint of Kensington Publishing Corporation.

Chant, Zoe. *Wildfire Griffin*. Copyright © 2018 by Zoe Chant. Independently published.

Clark, Mia. *Stepbrother with Benefits 1*. Copyright © 2016 by Mia Clark. Published by Cherrylily.

Collins, Manda. *Duke with Benefits*. Copyright © 2017 by Manda Collins. Published by St. Martin's Paperbacks, an imprint of St. Martin's Press.

Dare, Tessa. *Say Yes to the Marquess*. Copyright © 2015 by Eva Ortega. Published by Avon Books, an imprint of HarperCollins Publishers.

Daws, Amy. *Blindsided*. Copyright © 2019 by Amy Daws. Independently published.

Eden, Cynthia. *Before Ben*. Copyright © 2019 by Cindy Roussos. Published by Hocus Pocus Publishing.

Ellis, Shelly. *To Love & Betray*. Copyright © 2017 by Shelly Ellis. Published by Dafina Books, an imprint of Kensington Publishing Corporation.

Estep, Jennifer. *Jinx*. Copyright © 2008 by Jennifer Estep. Published by Berkley Sensation, The Berkley Publishing Group, a division of Penguin Group (USA) Inc.

Fenske, Tawna. *Stiff Suit*. Copyright © 2019 by Tawna Fenske. Independently published.

Forester, Amanda. *Earl Interrupted*. Copyright © 2018 by Amanda Forester. Published by Sourcebooks Casablanca, an imprint of Sourcebooks, Inc.

Gardiner, Jenny. *Sleeping with Ward Cleaver*. Copyright © 2008 by Jenny Gardiner. Published by Love Spell, an imprint of Dorchester Publishing Company, Inc.

Gibson, Rachel. *I Do!* Copyright © 2015 by Rachel Gibson. Published by Avon Impulse, an imprint of HarperCollins Publishers.

Goldberg, Gary David (director). *Must Love Dogs*. Warner Brothers, 2005. Screenplay by Gary David Goldberg. Based on the novel by Claire Cook.

Grant, Pippa. *America's Geekheart*. Copyright © 2019 by Pippa Grant. Independently published.

Gray, Ginna. *The Prime Objective*. Copyright © 2009 by Ginna Gray. Published by MIRA Books, an imprint of Harlequin Enterprises.

Grey, Amelia. *The Earl Next Door*. Copyright © 2019 by Amelia Grey. Published by St. Martin's Paperbacks, an imprint of St. Martin's Press.

Hackett, Anna. *Heart of Eon*. Copyright © 2019 by Anna Hackett. Independently published.

Harmon, Elizabeth. *Pairing Off*. Copyright © 2015 by Elizabeth Harmon. Published by Carina Press, an imprint of Harlequin Enterprises.

Harper, Molly. *A Few Pecans Short of a Pie*. Copyright © 2019 by Molly Harper White. Published by Gallery Books, an imprint of Simon & Schuster, Inc.

Harrison, Emma. *Tourist Trap*. Copyright © 2006 by Emma Harrison. Published by Avon Books, an imprint of HarperCollins Publishers.

Hart, Staci. *With a Twist*. Copyright © 2015 by Staci Hart. Independently published.

Heller, J. B. *Catastrophe Magnet*. Copyright © 2022 by J. B. Heller. Independently published.

Hoffmann, E. T. A. *Nussknacker und Mausekönig. (The Nutcracker and the Mouse King.)* Originally published in German in 1816. Retold in French by Alexandre Dumas as *Histoire d'un Casse-Noisette* in 1844. First adapted as a ballet by Marius Petipa in 1892.

Hovland, Christina. *The Honeymoon Trap*. Copyright © 2018 by Christina Hovland. Published by Amara, an imprint of Entangled Publishing, LLC.

Hunter, Denise. *Honeysuckle Dreams*. Copyright © 2018 by Denise Hunter. Published by Thomas Nelson, an imprint of HarperCollins Publishers.

Jae. *Not the Marrying Kind*. Copyright © 2019 by Jae. Published by Ylva Publishing, a legal entity of Ylva Verlag, e.Kfr.

Jalaluddin, Uzma. *Ayesha at Last*. Copyright © 2018 by Uzma Jalaluddin. Published by Berkley, an imprint of Penguin Random House LLC.

Jeffries, Sabrina. *Never Seduce a Scoundrel*. Copyright © 2006 by Deborah Gonzales. Published by Pocket Star Books, a division of Simon & Schuster, Inc.

Kaufman, Amie and Spooner, Meagan. *These Broken Stars*. Copyright © 2013 by Amie Kaufman and Meagan Spooner. Published by Hyperion, an imprint of Disney Book Group.

Kelly, Diane. *Death, Taxes, and a Satin Garter*. Copyright © 2016 by Diane Kelly. Published by St. Martin's Paperbacks, an imprint of St. Martin's Press.

Kennedy, Elle. *Midnight Revenge*. Copyright © 2016 by Leeanne Kenedy. Published by Signet Eclipse, an imprint of New American Library, an imprint of Penguin Random House LLC.

Kinsella, Sophie. *Wedding Night*. Copyright © 2013 by Madhen Mediaworks LLP. Published by The Dial Press, an imprint of The Random House Publishing Group, a division of Random House, Inc.

Kriss, Julie. *Crashed*. Copyright © 2019 by Julie Kriss. Published by Five Doors Creative.

Kurland, Lynn. *Princess of the Sword*. Copyright © 2009 by Lynn Curland. Published by Berkley Sensation, The Berkley Publishing Group, a division of Penguin Group (USA) Inc.

Landish, Lauren. *Mr. Fiancé*. Copyright © 2017 by Lauren Landish. Independently published.

Lawson, Piper. *Play*. Copyright © 2018 by Piper Lawson Books. Independently published.

Lewis, Beverly. *The Secret*. Copyright © 2009 by Beverly M. Lewis. Published by Bethany House Publishers.

Linden, Caroline. *An Earl Like You*. Copyright © 2018 by P. F. Belsley. Published by Avon Books, an imprint of HarperCollins Publishers.

Lindenblatt, Stina. *Decidedly With Baby*. Copyright © 2017 by Stina Lindenblatt. Independently published.

Livingston, Bree. *Tru*. Copyright © 2021 by Bree Livingston. Independently published.

Lorret, Vivienne. *Daring Miss Danvers*. Copyright © 2014 by Vivienne Lorret. Published by Avon Impulse, an imprint of HarperCollins Publishers.

Ludwig, V. K. *Swipe Right for Husband*. Copyright © 2020 by V. K. Ludwig. Published by Ink Heart Publishing.

MacLean, Sarah. *The Day of the Duchess*. Copyright © 2017 by Sara Trabucchi. Published by Avon Books, an imprint of HarperCollins Publishers.

Mallery, Susan. *All Summer Long*. Copyright © 2012 by Susan Macias Redmond. Published by HQN Books, an imprint of Harlequin Enterprises.

Malone, Nana. *Royal Tease*. Copyright © 2018 by Nana Malone. Independently published.

Mann, Susan. *The Librarian and the Spy*. Copyright © 2017 by Susan Mann. Published by Zebra Books, an imprint of Kensington Publishing Corporation.

Maxted, Anna. *Getting Over It*. Copyright © 2000 by Anna

Maxted. Published by ReganBooks, an imprint of HarperCollins Publishers.

Mayer, Dale. *Taylor*. Copyright © 2019 by Dale Mayer. Published by Valley Publishing, Ltd.

McCahan, Heidi. *Love Flies In*. Copyright © 2015 by Heidi McCahan. Published by Snug Corner Cove Press.

McFarlane, Mhairi. *If I Never Met You*. Copyright © 2020 by Mhairi McFarlane. Published by William Morrow, an imprint of HarperCollins Publishers.

McGee, Stephenia H. *Her Place in Time*. Copyright © 2018 by Stephenia H. McGee. Published by The Vine Press.

Menon, Sandhya. *From Twinkle with Love*. Copyright © 2018 by Sandhya Kutty Falls. Published by Simon Pulse, an imprint of Simon & Schuster Children's Publishing Division.

Monroe, Max. *The Billionaire Book Club*. Copyright © 2019 by Max Monroe. Independently published.

Netzel, Stacey Joy. *Trust by Design*. Copyright © 2014 by Stacey Joy Netzel. Independently published.

Neuhold, K. M. *Rocket Science*. Copyright © 2019 by K. M. Neuhold. Independently published.

Noyes, E. J. *Gold*. Copyright © 2018 by E. J. Noyes. Published by Bella Books, Inc.

O'Keeffe, Kate. *The Right Guy*. Copyright © 2019 by Kate O'Keeffe. Published by Wild Lime Books.

Palmer, Diana. *Courageous*. Copyright © 2012 by Diana Palmer. Published by HQN Books, an imprint of Harlequin Enterprises.

Price, Jordan Castillo. *Quill Me Now*. Copyright © 2019 by Jordan Castillo Price. Published by JCP Books.

Putney, Mary Jo. *Not Quite a Wife*. Copyright © 2014 by Mary Jo Putney, Inc. Published by Zebra Books, an imprint of Kensington Publishing Corporation.

Quarles, Angela. *Must Love More Kilts*. Copyright © 2017 by Angela Trigg. Published by Unsealed Room Press.

Quinn, Jillian. *Dear Future Ex-Wife*. Copyright © 2020 by Jillian Quinn. Published by Penn Publishing.

Quinn, Julia. *How to Marry a Marquis*. Copyright © 1999 by Julie Cotler Pottinger. Published by Avon Books, an imprint of HarperCollins Publishers.

Rai, Alisha. *Hate to Want You*. Copyright © 2017 by Alisha Rai. Published by Avon Books, an imprint of HarperCollins Publishers.

Ranald, Sophie. *Sorry Not Sorry*. Copyright © 2019 by Sophie Ranald. Published by Bookouture, an imprint of StoryFire, Ltd.

Rawlings, Naomi. *Tomorrow's First Light*. Copyright © 2019 by Naomi Mason. Published by Cedar Lake Press.

Riley, Fiona. *Unlikely Match*. Copyright © 2017 by Fiona Riley. Published by Bold Strokes Books, Inc.

Rochon, Farrah. *The Boyfriend Project*. Copyright © 2020 by Farrah Roybiskie. Published by Forever, an imprint of Grand Central Publishing.

Sahin, Brittney. *Finding His Mark*. Copyright © 2018 by Brittney Sahin. Published by EmKo Media.

Sands, Lynsay. *A Bite to Remember*. Copyright © 2006 by Lynsay Sands. Published by Avon Books, an imprint of HarperCollins Publishers.

Scarlett, Jessica. *A Lily in Disguise*. Copyright © 2020 by Jessica

Scarlett. Published by Redwing Publishing.

Score, Lucy. *No More Secrets*. Copyright © 2016 by Lucy Score. Published by That's What She Said Publishing, Inc.

Sinclair, Linnea. *An Accidental Goddess*. Copyright © 2006 by Linnea Sinclair Bernadino. Published by Bantam Books, an imprint of Bantam Dell, a division of Random House, Inc.

Smith, Amiee. *Strangely Amazing*. Copyright © 2018 by Amiee Smith. Published by AMY Publishing.

Spangler, Rachel. *Edge of Glory*. Copyright © 2017 by Rachel Spangler. Published by Bywater Books.

St. Michel, Elizabeth. *Surrender the Wind*. Copyright © 2016 by Elizabeth St. Michel. Independently published.

Stewart, Sylvie. *The Fix*. Copyright © 2018 by Sylvie Stewart. Published by Rolling Hearts Press.

Stockton, Kasey. *An Agreeable Alliance*. Copyright © 2021 by Kasey Stockton. Published by Golden Owl Press.

Sundin, Sarah. *The Sea Before Us*. Copyright © 2018 by Sarah Sundin. Published by Revell, a division of Baker Publishing Group.

Tara, Jane. *Forecast*. Copyright © 2007 by Jane Tara. Published by Love Spell, an imprint of Dorchester Publishing Company, Inc.

Taylor, Rachel. *My Convenient Marriage*. Copyright © 2019 by Rachel Taylor. Independently published.

Temple, Allison. *The Pick Up*. Copyright © 2018 by Allison Temple. Published by Riptide Publishing.

Vayden, Kristin. *Escaping His Grace*. Copyright © 2019 by Kristin Vayden. Published by Lyrical Press, an imprint of Kensington Publishing Corporation.

Weatherspoon, Rebekah. *So Right*. Copyright © 2016 by Rebekah Weatherspoon. Independently published.

Woods, Serenity. *Bride in Trouble*. Copyright © 2018 by Serenity Woods. Independently published.

Yarros, Rebecca. *The Last Letter*. Copyright © 2019 by Rebecca Yarros. Published by Amara, an imprint of Entangled Publishing, LLC.

ALSO BY
SIRI CALDWELL

fiction

THE MERMAID HYPOTHESIS

MISTLETOE MISHAP

DEAL-BREAKER

ANGEL'S TOUCH

EARTH ANGEL

ABOUT THE AUTHOR

Siri Caldwell has devoted much of her career to wrangling metadata (keywords, titles, abstracts, etc.) related to scientific publications, so when she turned to writing romance novels, then indie publishing, it was natural for her to obsess over how to optimize her novels' metadata. *Irresistible Blurbs: How to Write a Book Description Romance Readers Will Love* arose from that quest.

Visit her online at www.siricaldwell.com

www.ingramcontent.com/pod-product-compliance
Lightning Source LLC
Chambersburg PA
CBHW050353280326
41933CB00010BA/1439